Judith
Hutchings

ALL FOR LOVE
A Star original

October '76

ALL FOR LOVE

Dawn Langley Simmons

A STAR BOOK
published by
W. H. ALLEN

A Star Book
Published in 1975
by W. H. Allen & Co. Ltd.
A division of Howard & Wyndham Ltd.
44 Hill Street, London W1X 8LB

Printed in Great Britain by
Richard Clay (The Chaucer Press) Ltd., Bungay, Suffolk

ISBN 0 352 39815 9

For
my daughter
NATASHA
when she is
old enough to understand

In her first passion woman loves her lover,
  In all the others all she loves is love,
Which grows a habit she can ne'er get over,
  And fits her loosely—like an easy glove, . . .

Lord Byron, Canto III

With grateful thanks for permission given me by Mary Wilson (Mrs Harold Wilson) to quote her poem, 'The Hedonist.'

I also thank Dr Mattie Russell, Curator of Manuscripts, William R. Perkins Library, Duke University, Durham, North Carolina for permission to use extracts from the *Collected Papers of Dawn Pepita Simmons* (Dawn Langley-Simmons).

D.L.S.

Book One

CHAPTER ONE

For reasons of safety, I had my baby in a hospital in Philadelphia. When I brought her home to Charleston in South Carolina, we arrived in a heavy thunderstorm. There was nobody to meet us at the airport, and I decided to forget the expense and take a taxi home. First I called a friend, West Grant, to ask him to meet us at the house with an umbrella to protect the newborn child.

West was there to meet us and helped us transfer from the taxi to the cold, dank house. I could not help but give way to feelings of anger that my child should be coming home to this wreck of a place, with its peeling lead paint and broken windows, instead of to my beautiful mansion on Society Street, which had been sold from under me on the courtroom steps in Charleston. Was it so wrong to obey the teachings of the Church in which I was raised? Is Christian marriage so evil? Why do human beings behave like a pack of hungry wolves when one of their number does not conform?

One small bedroom had a gasfire set in the wall, and in that dismal room my child began her life at home. I was afraid that Rutherford-Davis, the chihuahua terrier, would be jealous, for *he* had been my baby up to that point. But I was delighted to see that Rutherford took to the baby at once, and so did Gussie Mae, the corgi!

There was no sign of my husband. Perhaps he was on

his boat, perhaps with a certain lady. I did not know. I had done everything I could to let him know that the baby was born, but I had no idea whether my messages had reached him.

For several days and nights we were alone in the house. Neither the front door nor the back locked properly. I counted the number of window-panes that had been broken while I had been in hospital giving birth to my child. Seventeen.

None the less, I was very happy in those first few days. I quite forgot how much I'd wanted a boy. I had decided to call the baby Natasha, and Margienell—after my beloved grandmother, Nell, who raised me, and for dear, beautiful Margie, my mother, my idol who died so young—and Paul, for her father, John-Paul. A long name for a tiny baby, but then I liked long names. As a matter of fact, John-Paul was always to call her 'Red', or 'Emma'. When we were courting I was 'Pet'. Later, it became 'Nigger'.

We had been home for ten days before John-Paul came to see us. He rushed in, took one look at the baby, and said, 'Whoever saw a blue-eyed nigger?' Natasha's hair was brown, like mine, and her milky blue eyes soon turned to a beautiful hazel colour.

I had hoped that, after all the suffering I'd been through, I would be allowed to enjoy my baby in peace. But it was not to be. Certain members of my husband's family decided that they wanted baby Natasha plus the royalties they imagined I was getting for my autobiography. They began sending a teenage relative over twice a day to inform me that the authorities had decided I was insane, and that they were coming to take my child from me and to carry me off to the State Hospital.

Three years later, all this sounds quite silly. Unbelievable that I should have got so worked up over such ridiculous threats! But for so long I had lived in such fear of my life. I had been harassed every day, shot at, knocked many times to the sidewalk, had my shoulder broken, nearly starved to death. I was a foreigner in a strange country. My adoptive mother in England was dying. Many of the 'friends' in America who had enjoyed my money and gifts now thought my usefulness was over, for I could buy them no more furniture or appliances. Besides, I had discovered that the laws of South Carolina did not always work to my advantage! So many terrible things had happened to me with the law's consent—to this day I have not seen a written accounting for the dispersal of my mansion and effects. And I have never heard of a woman in any civilized community being dispossessed, as I was, at twelve hours' notice.

I went to pieces over the threats to Natasha and myself, and for safety's sake I went to stay with a friendly neighbour. Every morning I used to go and feed my dogs, but one Tuesday I arrived to find the cold house oddly silent. None of the dogs barked as I approached, and none rushed to greet me as I let myself in. I stood in the hall, listening. I thought I heard a faint whimpering noise but I might have been mistaken. I stood there afraid to move, then screwed up enough courage to walk into the kitchen, where I thought the sound had come from.

I heard myself screaming. The back door was

swinging open, and the floor was littered with splinters of glass from the windows, scrunching as I stepped on them. I could see smears of blood on the furniture and walls, and in the middle of the floor a long dragging mark, like a children's slide in the ice, as though someone had skidded through the carpet of glass and under the kitchen table.

And there I found Jackie, my faithful German Shepherd. I crouched to look at her, and heard myself moaning. She seemed a mass of blood, with tiny fractures of glass cruelly larding the wounds. The whites of her eyes had turned a livid red, and the corners were encrusted with some sort of dark matter. She darted anxious looks towards me and away again, as though she was afraid I would be angry with her for letting the intruder in.

And then, for the first time in all the harassment since Natasha was born, I broke down and cried. 'Dear God, dear God, why has thou forsaken me?' I heard myself repeating as I half sat, half knelt, on that kitchen floor, weeping for myself and my child, and for the world down all the days since I was born. . . .

*   *   *

When I was born there was much confusion about whether I should be registered as a boy or girl. The ignorant midwife present finally decided 'male'. It took nearly thirty years to rectify her mistake.

The matron of a famous London hospital recently told me that a child of uncertain sex is almost always registered as a boy, but that in many cases this practice leads only to frustration and to misery. Dr James F. Glenn, Chief of Urology at Duke University, North Carolina has written:

Parents of children born with genital defects should not waste a day in having tests done that will lead to the establishment of the child's most suitable sex identity. The diagnosis and the decision of whether the child should be male or female can be made as early as the first week of life. The younger the better, to prevent the many psychological problems that can arise.

Dr Charles E. Shopfner, Professor of Radiology at the University of Missouri School of Medicine, declares:

If there is any doubt at all that the child is a boy or a girl, an X-ray examination of the internal genital passages should be made that very day.

Oh, if only Dr Shopfner had been my midwife! Looking back though, I doubt whether my child-mother, Margie, would have allowed her baby to be X-rayed. Even vaccination was against her religious convictions.

Sweet, darling Margie, who all her life was so put upon and hurt. She was so fragile and beautiful; they said that when she was giving birth to me she looked like a large china doll in bed. For a long time she had lived in a world of her own, a world peopled by witches and goblins, but into this world of fantasy and make-believe came the only man she would ever live with or love. No amount of family or friendly reasoning could dissuade her: she *must* marry him, just as—much later—I knew that I must marry John-Paul.

The boy's name was Jack Copper, who lived in the neighbouring Sussex village of Burwash. Their passionate love bordered on the thin line of hate. Although entirely unsuited, they were tied to one another by some strange and terrible knot, and, obstinately obeying the Church's law, she would never sever it. A doctor once told her: 'You cannot live with each other, neither can you live without each other.'

I was born out of wedlock, though my parents had married by the time my sister, Fay, was born some years later. For most of the nine months that I was coming, Margie shut herself up in her bedroom. A brutal male relative had kicked her in the stomach. Years later, a leading Harley Street specialist gave it as his opinion that I should have been one of twins, but this was apparently thwarted by the kick.

My natural father found a job with Harold Nicolson and Vita Sackville-West who needed, besides a chauffeur, a man-of-all trades to work for them in the then derelict castle they had bought at Sissinghurst. But my parents were to live in, and they were allowed to take only one child with them. Fay was the chosen one, so I was farmed out with my grandmother, who inherited with me the deep secret that I wasn't quite as I should be. Until I was five, and had to go to school, I believed that I was a little girl. I think that my grandmother must have spoken about me to my first teacher, Miss Huckvale, who had also been Margie's teacher, for she was very kind to me. The family all called me Dinkie—

which my sister and one of my aunts call me to this day. At school I was called Gordon, the name chosen for me by my grandmother after the gallant defender of Khartoum. I had a horror of violence, and the story of the unfortunate general being speared to death and then having his head cut off was repulsive. I hated my name and poor decapitated General Gordon.

All the time I attended Cross-in-Hand School I never remember using the lavatories. My grandmother had told me I mustn't. My genital organs were deformed. To be blunt, there was only a penis of sorts. I was terrified that the other boys would find out and—though I often had to torture myself for hours at a time—find out they never did! At lunchtime, and after school finished at four o'clock, I ran home to Havana and the privacy of our own bathroom!

Havana was my escape. How I loved that bungalow, which my grandmother had named from a cigar-box. In those days there was a little wood next door and beyond that Tilsmore Recreation Ground bordering miles of heather and trees. There one could always escape from reality. In my case I would write little poems and stories for 'Uncle Tom' and his 'Little League of Kindness' in the *Sussex Express and County Herald*.

V. Sackville-West read the first poem of mine that 'Uncle Tom' published. It went like this:

Oh if I could only be
In my cottage by the sea
Not by a noisy quay
But by a quiet lea
Oh, if I could only be
In my cottage by the sea.

Even then I was looking for peace and security, something that has, it seems, always managed to elude me.

V. Sackville-West was always very kind to me. I used to spend part of my school holidays at Sissinghurst, and she was never too busy to read anything I had written. I was never afraid of the tall, handsome, hatted woman in riding breeches whose own tragedy was that, had she been born a man, she would have inherited her beloved Knowle. I have often wondered whether, like my later friend Carson McCullers, the American novelist, Vita recognized me as a woman? Virginia Woolf's novel *Orlando* was about V. Sackville-West, thinly disguised as the hero who changed sex during the course of the story. If only Vita had lived to see Dinkie, as she also insisted upon calling me, become a latter-day Orlando!

Harold Nicolson was also very kind. When I grew up and went to live in America I never came home without bringing back a bright tie or shirt for him to wear at weekends at Sissinghurst.

Margie never liked Vita's Sissinghurst; it was her prison. But I loved it. In *Portrait of a Marriage*, Vita's son, Nigel Nicolson, has described his parents' amazing relationship and has recounted Vita's extra-marital activities with other women. Of course my sister and I grew up with that knowledge, though we never talked about it beyond the confines of Sissinghurst. However, it was a bit hard on beautiful Margie with her jet black hair. I remember an afternoon when one of Vita's lovers, having imbibed a little too freely, walked into Margie's house by mistake. I can see Margie now, standing like some miniature Britannia at the top of the stairs ready to defend her honour with a Zulu shield and spear.

By the time I was ten I had written my first novel, called *The Green Orchid*. In a way it was autobiographical. I was the ugly duckling daughter with the beautiful mother. In this case I called 'myself' Stanley.

I loved my sister very much, and yet I envied her, for our father loved girls and hated boys. I never once remember him lifting me on to his knee to love me. He never bought me so much as a sock when I was a child! When his work took him abroad he would bring back gifts for everyone but me. Pretending that I was not forgotten, Margie would run to a shop and buy me some toy as though it was from Jack.

Once a year, in the early days, she came to see us at Havana. I stayed home from school on such red-letter occasions and my schoolfriends would say that Gordon's other mother had come. No man can serve two mistresses, and I was always torn between Margie and the grandmother whom I called 'Mum'.

When I was very young and had golden curls, my Aunty Babs would take me to Eastbourne and buy me special clothes. But then she went away and had children of her own, leaving me alone with my grandmother.

Every evening and at weekends, we lived in our own little world of books, writing and pets. The most exciting thing that ever happened was when the Duchess of Windsor paid a brief visit to Sussex. I spent all my savings—the then enormous sum of seven shillings and sixpence—to buy her a bunch of carnations.

I was also chosen—'because he looks so much like a

girl'—to play the heroine's role in the local wolf-cub play: *Mariposa Bong—The Pirate's Daughter*. I really lived the part in my crinoline, poke bonnet and cork-screw curls! As a child, the only clothes that really interested me were those worn by Margie on her special visits. In dress she was perfection! It's funny what one remembers . . . her long jade ear-rings . . . embroidered daisies on a scarlet gown . . . her favourite amber beads. Meantime, I could not tell one motor car from another, and 'masculine' sports were anathema.

Instead of pyjamas I was made to wear a white flannelette nightgown. I shall never forget it. Nor shall I easily forget the nerve-shattering night when, as a seven-year-old, I was taken 'for a treat' to stay with friends. I had to sleep with their teenage son, who had a grand time mocking the nightie. I was terrified of his discovering the secret it concealed, and I counted the hours till we got home again.

On Saturdays we always went to Spicers, the ancient Tudor house in Cade Street where my Uncle George Ditch and Aunty Liz lived. From the age of thirty, Uncle George had been paralysed from the waist down. One of his hands was also badly crippled. I've often told John-Paul the story of Uncle George and what happened to him when he deceived my aunt: instead of going shopping as he had told her, he went rabbit shooting, tripped over his gun and was ruined for life.

He retired with Aunty Liz to Spicers. He never complained. If he could not go out into the world then he would let the world come to him. We never knew who was going to be seated at the tea table, a gypsy or a Cabinet minister. Everybody, even I, was encouraged

to join in the conversation. Because of his own disable-
ment, Uncle George felt a natural affinity with others
physically afflicted—and with no one more so than the
little 'nephew', whom I am sure he knew was really a
little girl.

How I enjoyed going to Spicers, with its winding
passages and secret rooms. Once I arrived to find a
crowd outside and, crawling through their legs, found
myself looking at a large man, wearing nothing but
white pantaloons, cooking on a portable stove on the
lawn. On further investigation I found that the Egyp-
tian Ambassador was calling. He had brought his own
cook.

Like Blanche in Tennessee Williams' play *A Streetcar
Named Desire*, I have always depended on the kindess of
strangers. Often I have been bitterly disappointed. My
grandmother protected me—just as my cousin, the
painter Isabel Lydia Whitney, would protect me later
in my life when I was living in New York—each of
them a buffer against the cruelty of the outside world.
Knowing that because of my natal defect I would never
be able to marry—at least, not as Gordon; and not even
in our wildest dreams could either of us have foreseen
Dawn—my grandmother took steps to make sure that
in other respects I would, as an adult, be able to hold
my own. Although funds were limited, she made it her
business to persuade some of the best minds in the
village to tutor me. This, reinforcing the attentions of my
devoted teachers at school, substituted for the college
and university she could never have hoped to afford.
(It still amuses me that now, after writing some twelve
books, American professors who invite me to lecture for

them will blithely ask what university I attended!)

During my actual schooldays I had to take periods of rest when, in fact, I felt perfectly well. But it was necessary to live out the lie that I was not strong enough to take part in physical exercises like the other 'boys'. By the time I was four my grandmother had already taught me to read and write. When I was six I was one of twelve prize-winners in a children's story-writing contest organized by a national magazine. I told the tale of a mother rabbit who built herself a raft that was pulled by two large kippers.

In time my cats and dogs took the place of the dolls and stuffed toys I had first played with. When they died it was like losing human friends. At ten, the first of a long line of puppies called Josephine died, and I cried every day for a month. To this day I remember her in my prayers, for it says in the Bible that not a sparrow falls to the ground but God knows about it.

With the coming of the teenage years the worrisome bleedings began, and more than ever I realized I was not like other 'boys'. I had to enlarge the lie. My hair I cut extra short, shaved—with little success, for there was nothing there to warrant much effort—and wore the most masculine tweed jackets I could find. The other fellows were interesting themselves in the opposite sex, but I couldn't care less. I liked girls as friends, nothing more. With boys I was never at ease. I walked alone, and as a consequence I was thought odd and stand-offish. God knows I wanted to belong, to be one with my 'normal' contemporaries, but fate had long since decreed otherwise.

I enjoyed my religion, although a priest once told me—and I have good reason to agree with him, especially after my experiences in the American Deep South —that the nearer some people get to the altar, the more unchristian and wicked they become. The village church was always an important part of my life, as it was of my grandmother's. I joined the choir at the age of seven; at sixteen I was still a soprano! It was mortifying! One Sunday evening I hung up my cassock and surplice for the last time, though my voice never broke. (In 1974 I took Natasha back to St Bartholomew's Church at Cross-in-Hand and, standing by my old choir stall, I could only give silent thanks to the God who had seen fit to release me from my years of physical bondage.)

Of course I was lonely, but I did have my grandmother. Her advice was to work. I must write, write, write. I knew that one day I would be an author; that then I would be able to write my womanly books in the first person and in effect live a substitute feminine life within the outer shell that was Gordon. Jack Cooper mocked the idea that I might one day write a book. His laughter only made me the more determined that I should. Years later, however, Jack seemed to enjoy his share of the royalty cheques.

The teenage years in no way dimmed my love of home life. Havana was the pivot of my existence, yet it was not to last long. Within one short year it was all swept away. First Uncle George Ditch died. His last words to me were, ironically, 'Dinkie, you have been a good girl'. I had been right then: with the special sensitivity of the afflicted he had known the truth all along. Then my grandmother began to fail before my eyes. She had known for a long time that she was ill, but had told no one because she didn't want to be a trouble. By the time it became obvious, it was too late to help her. That vibrant soul now sat for long periods in an armchair, her swollen left arm painful to see. I had always lived in dread of something happening to her. As a child I feared she might be run over by a car, and I'd had nightmares about it.

Margie, still feminine and beautiful, arrived to help nurse her. Everybody had assured me that my grandmother would recover, but one afternoon I heard Margie talking to a relative. 'You know how hard it is to get anyone to nurse a cancer case. She doesn't want to go to hospital, so Dinkie and I must do it by ourselves.'

I turned and fled into the woods, where I threw myself down in the heather and sobbed aloud. Grandmother was going to leave me alone, with nobody to share my secret. Nobody else except her and Uncle George Ditch had ever really cared.

I do not like to remember those terrible three months. For years afterwards I would relive them in my dreams, always seeing the bathtub filled with bloody washing. Yet we nursed her together, Margie and I. It was a woman's job that I felt privileged to share.

My grandmother died one November night, the ground white with frost and drenched in moonlight. An unearthly blueish light appeared around my bedroom fireplace. Her identical twin, whom I knew as Aunty Doom, seemed to sense that her sister was dying, for when I delivered the note telling of her sister's passing I peeped through the letter-box and there she sat, huddled at the foot of the stairs . . . waiting for the news she knew in her heart was on its way. Poor Aunty Doom: she herself died some years later, at the exact same minute of her twin's death. My cousin Mary, her daughter-in-law, told me that in death she grew a moustache and looked just like a man.

We buried my grandmother above the young husband who had died so many years before. It was a yellow, misty day; the funeral cars had orange lights to pierce the fog. I chose for her a plain, unpolished coffin surmounted by a large raised bronze cross. I tried to find a suitable text to write on my floral heart of purple violets but all I could think of were Christ's terrible words from His cross: 'My God, my God, why hast thou forsaken me?'

For a time I really felt that he had. I was turned out of Havana and saw the things we loved laid out for auction on the ground at Heathfield Market. It was snowing. Margie had returned to Sissinghurst and I had nowhere to go until a dear old lady, a true friend, let me have a room in her little house. I remember that it had real William Morris wallpaper. The local curate kindly lent me a tea kettle.

Then and there I decided to go to America, where nobody would know me. Gordon was to be swallowed up in merciful obscurity.

CHAPTER TWO

The years between Gordon the teenager and Dawn the woman were certainly eventful, but they are not of signal importance to my love story. The most important thing, by far, was my adoption by the famous, warm-hearted and much-loved actress Margaret Rutherford and her husband Stringer Davis. Why this enchanting pair of childless lovers chose me as one of their four adopted children is explained by Mother Rutherford in her autobiography. In the dark days ahead of me, their loving support was something I came to rely on almost too much.

I did go to America. There were, for example, lonely but happy days teaching on an Ojibway Indian reservation, which resulted in my life-long interest in the North American Indian peoples, and in four books, all of them praised by an American–Indian conference at the University of Minnesota for their factual accuracy and recommended for use in libraries across America.

At one point I worked as a reporter with the *Winnipeg Free Press*—I think this was my favourite job of all—and then I was off to the small city of Nevada, Missouri, where the wire services hailed me as 'the only male Society editor in the state'. I had forty women country correspondents under me!

Then came New York and my life at 12 West Tenth Street, home of my cousin, the painter Isabel Lydia

Whitney. Her protection of me was most desperately needed, for although this period was my most productive as a writer, it was also my worst in terms of health.

The bleedings were so regular that I came to expect them every month. In addition, there were constant ruptures in the rectal area. For an entire year I could not even go to the movies. Despite wearing all sorts of preventive pads and clothing, the blood was constantly seeping through.

One morning I woke to find my legs and stomach so swollen that one doctor asked if I had recently been in the tropics, thinking perhaps that I might have contracted some terrible disease. Nobody seemed to know what was the matter. I was granted the Grace Church bed in St Luke's Hospital, New York City, because I had written a religious play, a modern morality called *Saraband for a Saint*, which had been presented in St Martin's Episcopal Church in Harlem. I lay in hospital for several weeks. One leading newspaper columnist wrote that I was dying of cancer, but I wasn't. Finally, the swelling having subsided I went home. My Harley Street specialist thinks I went through all the stages of a false pregnancy, like some poor old she-dog who wants puppies but hasn't got a husband.

At this point I should mention that I had been befriended by one of the finest human beings I have ever met. Raymond Smith, of Atlantic City, New Jersey, was a Black soloist at St Martin's. He used to take me for drives into the countryside. Years afterwards, as Dawn, I went to Atlantic City, where he then lived, to ask his advice about marrying my John-Paul. Raymond had always given me good counsel.

Did Raymond first stir in me my womanly emotions? Until then I had been like a vegetable. Sex was only a word; it had no intimate meaning. It was for John-Paul to initiate me into the world of physical love.

As at Havana I cherished the privacy and security of the Whitney house. But everything comes to an end. Isabel contracted leukaemia. Since I had promised Isabel that she would die at home, I ran something like a three-ring circus in that museum-like setting, replete with antiques and works of art. Isabel died and it was left to me to close her eyes.

One is often cautioned not to act in haste following a bereavement, yet, perversely, I did just that. I had been very intrigued with the old houses I had seen on my travels in South Carolina, and after complicated nego-tiations bought a derelict old mansion, the Dr Joseph Johnson House, located on Society Street in the Ansonborough district of Charleston.

It was the biggest mistake I ever made, though I got a fine husband and a little daughter as a delayed bonus.

In Charleston, a very pro-British city, I had three valuable assets. I was a well-to-do author, I was British and I was unmarried. Oh those dreadful society dinners at which I would be sitting next to somebody who needed a husband, and in whom I hadn't the slightest interest—mental or physical. Thank God I could pre-tend to be an eccentric stay-at-home, contented to write books.

V. Sackville-West sent me a plan for the garden; I filled the house with a collection of antiques, and it was opened to the public for visits as part of 'Historic Charleston Foundation' tours.

A formidable housekeeper and butler solved the staff problems. Then, one morning, the housekeeper arrived at the house to find me lying in a pool of blood. She called an ambulance and rushed me to the hospital where they pumped out what they called 'stale blood'. Nurse Mary Kaye Hardee, who was on duty then, has ever since spoken up when anybody has cast doubt on the veracity of my story. 'Now wait a minute,' she says. 'I was there in the beginning.'

I had specialized in writing the biographies of the First Ladies of America, and at the time was engaged in working on a book about Lady Bird Johnson and her daughter. It was a very pleasant assignment. Mrs Johnson was so nice to me, and I was anxious to do a good job. But I felt, oh, so ill. I looked grey in the face, my hair grew and grew, there were great changes in my breasts. (I could no longer wear a sports jacket properly, for it would not hang straight.) But eventually Mrs Johnson's biography was completed. It was to be Gordon's swan-song.

In desperation I arranged an appointment with Dr Duncan Pringle of Charleston at whose house I had often been a guest. She was very sympathetic and sent me to a gynaecologist at a local hospital. 'I think you know what I am going to tell you,' he began. 'X-rays were taken, a six-and-one-half inch vaginal passage has been discovered. Things must be put right—and quickly!' The hospital authorities informed the Charleston police and the mayor of the city that this was a medical problem. I was advised to get a woman relative or friend to buy some women's clothing. Having nobody to undertake this assignment for me, I had to rely on the choice of a local store. Really, they sold me the most impossible garments! Probably all the things they couldn't get rid of to anyone else!

I wrote home to Margie, Aunty Babs, Mother Rutherford and Father Stringer. They were all simply wonderful, and urged me to come home, but I decided against it. I would see it through on my own, and try to keep it as private as possible. After all, it was a medical problem. Before the surgical operation itself, there was a lengthy period of psychiatric treatment in the Women's Clinic at John Hopkins Hospital in Baltimore, one of the finest medical centres in America. Hormone treatment was beginning to help me now. Even the shape of my face was changing. Little by little, Gordon was fading into the distance and Dawn Pepita—the latter Spanish name taken in honour of V. Sackville-West, whose gypsy grandmother's name it had been— was taking his place.

The actual physical examinations by surgeons, gynae-cologists and urologists did not worry me. Although as a child I had hated such attention, now it bothered me not at all. Even being photographed nude was not the ordeal I feared it would have been. Hope was rising triumphant. I knew the eventual outcome!

I found all the oral tests and interviews tedious, but they were a necessary part of the procedure, and so had to be 'endured'. I must have repeated the story of my life a hundred times. One lady psychologist was keen to write my life story, but I declined gracefully. Surely, I thought, I of all people, should write that!

The question of dreams often came up. I have always been a great dreamer. I told them of a recurrent dream in which I saw myself walking out of Cross-in-Hand Church, dressed as a bride in white lace with the petals of the wild cherry tree falling about me like confetti. The groom was there, but where his face should have been there was just a blank. This seemed to intrigue them all.

Questions about my sex life were easily handled, for until that time sex had been of little or no interest to me. After all, I did not feel I was capable of enjoying it in any form. I had not experienced sexual intercourse, because I couldn't. Now, however, the frequent burnings in my breast were stirring strange fires within me.

My doctors were all optimistic that in the days ahead I would meet a life-companion, one who would give me the peace and security that I had so long been denied. They thought I needed marriage. Nearly thirty, sexually naïve, and a writer! How the combination made them smile.

They said the surgery would be a cleaning-up process. The vaginal passage had to be opened and 'lips' created. So successful were the surgeons that if I have to undress for a doctor now he never suspects unless I volunteer the information. I do not remember being unduly frightened the night before Gordon died . . . only grateful. I fell asleep, then awoke in the morning anxious to sleep once more. I remember the sunshine. And I remember also a friend wishing me 'Happy Birthday', as I went to my new life.

I recovered consciousness, but all I wanted was to sleep again. . . . I drifted between wakefulness and sleep . . . there was no pain, just a dull ache.

When I awoke there seemed to be tubes everywhere, one of them attached to the upper wrist of my left hand. A clear, saline solution dripped from a bottle slung over my bed, through a tube that penetrated the operation area. The problem of passing water was solved by a catheter fixed into the bladder, and this enabled my urine to be drained into a large plastic bag. Its volume was carefully measured every few hours. I had a great craving for fruit juices, with which I was liberally supplied.

A mole under my right breast had been removed; in its place were several stitches. 'It must have been a big one', said a cheerful nurse as she dressed the wound.

The dead useless flesh that for thirty years had passed as Gordon's penis was gone. Instead there were newly-created vaginal lips, which if successful—as they turned out to be—would allow me to play the woman's role in marriage.

The vagina was taped, but slowly, slowly my hands worked down to touch that blessed second mouth.

I recovered quickly. Within three days, while the drainage tubes were still attached, I was sitting up and at work again. I was writing a biography entitled *A Rose for Mrs Lincoln*. It seemed so fitting to be at work on the story of another human being who had been so emotionally disturbed and misunderstood.

Then came the time for me to return to Charleston, there to face a bevy of television cameramen. I was wearing a navy blue and white mini-skirted outfit. The local newscaster said: 'Here is the news . . . and boy, do we have news for you tonight.'

The operation had taken place on 23 September 1968. News was sent to Mother Rutherford, and on 30 September I received her blessing.

My dear Pepita,

So you have got through the final crisis! I am so glad to know of this. Now you will feel no unwelcome restraint. How right you were to allow your operation to be public—right and brave! You are in the hands of God, and he will have you in His care, as He has done all the time. May you ever be blessed—as indeed you will be.

To this Father Stringer had added: 'P.S. At any rate, you can always remember "Gordon" as a very brave man.'

CHAPTER THREE

Now that I was Dawn, I suppose I could have slipped away and lived quietly, far from Charleston, where 'Gordon's' drama had reached its happy climax. But I did not want to run away. Besides, I had a large investment in my home, into which I had poured energy and money to restore its former beauty. Being British, I also liked the sense of privacy that my walled garden gave me. Moreover, there was still my work, for I had no intention of giving up writing. My fan-mail had increased a hundredfold, and it came not just from readers. So many people wrote, not only to me, but also to Mother Rutherford and Father Stringer, telling of their own personal sexual tragedies. It made me realize that I had never really been alone in the personal dilemma that was now no more than a bad dream. When people asked for advice on what they should do, I could only reply: 'See your doctor; there may still be hope.'

As for Dawn, she had, so it seemed, to make up for lost time. The doctors were worrying me to go out and meet people of my own age . . . to have a few experiences with men. 'You must gain confidence with the opposite sex,' they told me.

They might well have saved their breath to cool their porridge. For destiny had already singled out my man. Like Margie before me, for better or worse I would love him blindly—and for ever.

His name was John-Paul Simmons. Proud, black, extrovert, he was the fourth son of a respected Baptist deacon. One of eleven children, he had walked out of school when he was twelve. His great loves were the river and tales of the sea. He was also the bravest man, Black or White, I ever met in the American South. In openly loving me, a White woman, he ran the gravest risks. As it was to turn out, of course, so did I, in loving him.

He later told me that he first saw me one evening as I was walking Jackie, my German Shepherd, and Josephine, my chihuahua terrier. We were by a large fountain.

One day, after working all evening I was interrupted by my maid, who left the house in a huff because her date had not turned up that evening. Ten minutes later the doorbell rang and I went to answer it. There he was, John-Paul, whom I later described in my diary as 'a thick-set, smiling man, his cap pulled carelessly over part of his forehead. . . . He has a nice neck.'

He just looked at me standing there in the ankle-length robe in which I liked to write. . . . He did not ask for my maid. Perhaps he knew that he had come home. It was as if I had known him long ago . . . long, long ago in a dim distant past . . . perhaps in some other life—I don't know. My legs shook, and as we used to say at school were cramped with 'pins and needles'.

We touched hands and he was gone. (One day he was to tell a reporter from the *Washington Daily News*: 'She was the whitest and most sickly-looking woman I ever did see, yet I knew from that minute she was mine . . . that no man but me was ever going to touch her.)

Back indoors I wanted a drink . . . although apart

33

from the occasional glass of sherry or champagne I usually never drank!

Then I saw the portrait of my great-great grandmother, the Spanish Condesa, hanging on the wall of the lower drawing-room and I thought of something she had said: 'A woman is like a fruit. If it is not picked it will fall when it is ripe.'

How hard Dawn fell!

John-Paul was employed as a mechanic at a near-by garage. The morning after he had called, he telephoned me. Alexander, my ancient butler, really quite crumbling, was most upset. 'It wasn't even a White man's voice,' he complained.

Then as I walked in my garden a young man brought me a message. 'John-Paul wants to make you happy; he will never hurt you,' he said. It was beginning to sound like Jane Austen. How Isabel Whitney, the last of the New York romantics, would have loved it!

That night, as I was eating my supper from a tray and watching the six o'clock news on television, I heard a commotion in the kitchen. Next, John-Paul, wearing blue overalls and covered with grease, his cap still on his head, crashed into the sitting-room, knocked the tray from my lap, and dropped an enormous bunch of flowers in its place. They were dripping wet!

'I will never leave you again,' he said . . . and in a way he never did.

It was hopeless to fight him. Of course, I felt flattered—what old maid of thirty wouldn't? But I think that Charleston society never really believed I would marry him. Many people, both Black and White, tried to stop

34

us. But John-Paul, with characteristic obstinacy, decided that we should wed right there. (Looking back, it's a wonder neither of us was killed. . . . Somebody did take a shot at him.) We were subjected to a most painful interview with a Black Baptist minister whose words have since infuriated thousands of liberal men and women of all races. The record of this incident in my diary reads:

John-Paul believes that the minister had made up his mind not to marry us before he ever met us. Rumour must be right when it reports that he is running for political office and is afraid of upsetting the White hierarchy. What to me is so immoral was the man's suggestions that we should live together in sin and not be married. I was seething that one of John-Paul's own race should put more rocks in our already rocky path. I tried to be dignified, saying, 'In England we have a word for a woman like that . . . a fancy woman . . . and I've been through too much to be that.'

Ironically, on the way home we met the Reverend William Singleton, Assistant Pastor of Shiloh Afro-Methodist Episcopal Church. We told him our story and, great man that he was, he immediately offered to join us in matrimony.

Next day it was the White folks' turn. Three dear old ladies, with the yellowing parchment look of fading Southern belles, called bearing gifts—a water-melon for John-Paul and an apple pie for me. Why couldn't I, they asked, be like the White lady who had married into Charleston society but had always loved her Black butler? Now old, and a widow, she was left in her crumbling mansion with her lover. They sounded like something out of Tennessee Williams. After they left I said I was going to throw the water-melon into the trash can. 'Not on your life,' replied John-Paul. 'That's good fruit and I'm going to eat it.'

The psychiatrists at John Hopkins, hearing that I was to marry a Black man, expressed forebodings, saying that I had complicated my problems threefold. So John-Paul left Charleston to ask twenty-five very eminent doctors for my hand.

As I sat outside while he was interviewed, I caught the sound of spontaneous laughter. When he came out I inquired what had caused such merriment. 'Well,' he began, sounding very puritanical for a man who was always boasting about all the women he'd had, 'Do you know what they asked me? They asked me if I had slept with you.'

'What did you say,' I asked.

'None of your goddam business,' he'd replied.

He has always been like that, brutally honest, even with the Archbishop of Canterbury. That is why people like him.

The doctors sent us a message. 'Marry . . . you are a very brave young couple. We only hope you will not be assassinated.'

We were engaged in New York City. I wore a gown of white chiffon and silver sequins—the first time I had ever chosen a dress for myself. We appeared on the eleven o'clock news where there was a marvellous shot of John-Paul kissing my bare shoulder.

He was twenty-one years old on 10 January 1969. He

36

had always said he would not marry until he came of age. The doctors had told him that, sexually, he was an old man compared to me. I was getting a little nervous, as I didn't think I knew as much as I should about the subject, so I wrote to Mother Rutherford and Father Stringer for advice. Father Stringer sent me a booklet on marriage and sex which the minister had given them after their own wedding in Buckinghamshire. He did caution me, however, that it hadn't been much help to either of them. They were not much better off the morning after their wedding than they had been the night before. 'Perhaps, dear heart,' my Mother Rutherford wrote in one of inimitable postscripts, 'you will have better luck. I hope so.'

On the night of his twenty-first birthday I woke up to find John-Paul breathing into my face. 'We are getting married tomorrow,' he said. I replied, 'You must have been drinking.' President Nixon was being inaugurated for his first term of office on the following day, so even I could not oblige my husband-to-be! The temporary court house on Cumberland Street was closed and we could not apply for the marriage licence until the day after. When we did, the Judge, Gus H. Pearlman, who is Jewish, said to me: 'I have always been in the minority; now welcome to the minority!'

When we got home John-Paul had to use force to evict a television cameraman crouched on the lower piazza.

A *Newsweek* story claimed that by deciding to marry we had rocked the 'Cradle of the Confederacy'. Certainly, our problems began immediately. The church where our wedding was to take place was threatened with bombing—John-Paul's mother said we would all be sweeping up in Heaven next day! And so we had to be married in my sitting-room. I used a French table that had once belonged to my great-grandmother, the Condesa, as a makeshift altar; I placed my beloved statue of St Teresa of Avila, patron of writers, upon it.

I wore the white lace gown that I had seen myself wearing so often in the old recurring dream. I had spotted it in the window of a store as I drove with John-Paul down Charleston's King Street in a red Thunderbird that I had bought him. The night before our wedding I dreamed the dream for the last time, and the bridegroom no longer had a blank for a face . . . I saw him now . . . my dear John-Paul.

Crowds gathered in the street outside, the house was thoroughly searched by detectives for bombs, there were countless police on duty. People kept saying that John-Paul would never turn up, but he did. His father, Deacon Joseph Simmons, gave me away, for at the last minute a local Black attorney had refused to perform this office, leaving me alone at the top of the stairs! Never mind, as I walked down they played 'The Battle Hymn of the Republic' on a gramophone—and what could be more truly American than that?

It hardly needs to be said that we had long since lost my maid, John-Paul's original date! As a matter of fact we had lost our butler, too, for the decrepit Alexander did not approve of our wedding. We engaged a new butler, named James Fickling, whom John-Paul called 'Ficky'. Mr James enjoyed the wedding. He drank so much champagne we couldn't get him to go home. Finally we had to take him ourselves, at four in the morning, and dawn was breaking as we returned home. There was I in a blue chiffon nightgown complete with sequins. This made our wedding bliss extremely scratchy. John-Paul was quite upset. On top of this we were exhausted! We had earlier phoned Margie, who was in Hawkhurst Cottage Hospital with pneumonia, and Mother Rutherford and Father Stringer, who said we were to remember that they had four adopted children but were yet to get a grandchild.

They had reckoned without Mr James and my sequinned nightgown. I went to clean my teeth, and when I came out of the bathroom John-Paul was snoring!

He was furious next morning, and never afterwards lost the opportunity of reminding Mr James that he had spoilt his 'first night'.

The doctors had told John-Paul that they'd done all they could for me, but could not be there on the wedding night itself. It was up to him to make me warm or frigid. He could either make me like sex or hate it. A month after the wedding they asked him how he'd made out when the occasion arrived.

'Well, it was like this,' said John-Paul, not letting on that it was really the second night. 'I found out that she couldn't drink. One sherry and she's all right . . . two and she's under the table . . . *So I gave her five*.'

Ten days later I had to go into hospital for a routine operation that was designed simply to increase John-Paul's pleasure. If only he had undressed beforehand for the doctor . . . but, as Mother Rutherford later consoled me, 'Oh, these prudish Baptists'.

Of course, with typical Dawn Langley-Simmons luck

I had to fall down in the snow when leaving hospital, and hurt my leg. I was laid up for a month with my leg in traction. During that time John-Paul managed to blow up the kitchen with his cooking! Mr James never quite got over it all.

I'm sure you will agree that the early days of my marriage were not entirely without incident.

CHAPTER FOUR

Mother Rutherford told *Time* magazine that she didn't mind my marrying a Black man, but she did wish I wasn't marrying a Baptist. This was a bit hard on the Baptists! She was magnificent during all the hullabaloo that resulted from the announcement that I was going to marry my butler.

John-Paul was never my butler. He couldn't carry a cup and saucer across the room without dropping it. He was working as a mechanic with Simmons Garage on Church Street, Charleston, when I met him, and later, after we married, he owned his own shrimp boat. As Anthony Dawson, the actor and our child's godfather, said: 'He was a shrimper!' Another good friend commented, 'What would it have mattered if he was a butler, as long as he was a good butler?' However, truth is truth, and the person connected with the wire services in Charleston who made up this malicious lie obviously thought he would degrade us. Certainly the lie put down tenacious roots. Even Princess Margaret once asked me, 'Mrs Simmons, did you really marry your butler?'

Mother Rutherford was very upset that, because of the bomb threats, we had been wed in my sitting-room. She was furious when she heard about the Uncle Tom pastor who had said: 'Why can't you two just live together. You don't have to get married.' She wanted a proper church wedding in our own faith, the Church of England. She was also determined that expert medical opinion concerning my status should be made public knowledge.

Now my Mother Rutherford almost qualified as a British Institution. She commanded attention.

Upon arrival in London at the beginning of November, 1969, there was such a mob waiting to see us at Heathrow Airport, that John-Paul and I were guided out by another entrance. Mother Rutherford and Father Stringer met us at an hotel in the Strand. They immediately liked my John-Paul, and he responded fully to their love. Mother Rutherford took me to a leading gynaecologist and, on the strength of that visit, a statement from him appeared on the front page of the Sunday newspaper, *The People*, declaring that in his opinion I had been wrongly sexed as a baby, that I had always been a woman, and that I was quite capable of having a child.

Mother Rutherford and Father Stringer arranged that a Blessing of Marriage should take place the following Sunday, 9 November 1969, at the twelfth-century St Clement's Church, Hastings.

The ceremony was to be performed by the rector of St Clement's, a friend of ours, and the Reverend G. Savins, who had been vicar of All Saints, Old Heathfield, when I gave that church an Anglo-American Friendship window, which was unveiled by Mother Rutherford.

Special wedding invitations were quickly dispatched to relatives and friends. They read:

Mr J. Stringer Davis
and
Dame Margaret Rutherford Davis, O.B.E.,
request the honour of your presence
at the blessing of the marriage
of their adoptive daughter
Dawn Pepita Langley Hall
to
Mr John-Paul Simmons
at two-thirty o'clock
Sunday afternoon, November the ninth
Saint Clement's Church
Hastings, Sussex
and afterwards at the reception

All that week we had a frantic list of engagements
which included tea with the Archbishop of Canterbury,
a day of filming for a television commercial, a trip to
Sissinghurst to Margie's grave, a service in Westminster
Abbey. In the Abbey John-Paul made the classic remark, 'I can't understand it. Nobody is staring at us.'
There were piles of good wishes, letters, cards, tele-
grams and flowers from all over the country. We might
have been movie-stars, like my adoptive parents.

Mother Rutherford told us that Her Majesty the
Queen had been very sympathetic on hearing of our
sufferings in Charleston. My adoptive mother had been
to Buckingham Palace for lunch and afterwards had
been honoured with an invitation to the Queen's private
sitting-room where, among other things, they had
discussed my situation.

John-Paul and I specially enjoyed a visit we paid to
the television studios.

John-Paul watched the hairdresser and cosmetic expert at work on my face and suddenly cried: 'Don't make her too beautiful or somebody will take her away from me.' She replied, 'I've worked on many famous people, but that's the most beautiful thing any husband ever said to me!' Of course, I was close to tears at his words.

It poured with rain on the great day, but the Lord was with us, for by the time we were ready to leave for Sussex in a caravan of cars the rain had stopped.

We arrived at my Cousin Rosamanda's house in good time for a pre-wedding feast that was typical of Sussex: ham sandwiches, pickled onions, roast pork, roast beef, home-made custards and jellies. My Burgess cousins, from Kent, with their husbands and children, were also there to meet us. John-Paul was all the time protesting loudly about the marvellous shirt with ruffles that he was going to wear. (He actually carried it dangling from the end of a walking-stick as we went into Cousin Rosamunda's house.)

David Lee Stokes II, of Nashville, Tennessee, had made my second wedding gown. It was of heavy gold brocade and velvet, with large leg-o'-mutton sleeves. According to Mother Rutherford, it was very theatrical and Shakespearean. Most suitable.

I dressed in Cousin Rosamanda's bedroom. Believe it or not, her twin King Charles spaniels sniffed out a German press photographer hiding under the bed! There are no depths to which some people will not sink.

The hairdressers fixed my veil and pearl tiara so that it would be safe in the high wind that was blowing. I walked down the garden path to a waiting white-ribboned car as leaves swirled down from the trees. John-Paul had gone on ahead with my cousin Nigel Burgess, who was to be his best man. A good driver himself, he said that after the way Cousin Nigel drove his racing car through those narrow winding lanes he felt a nervous wreck when they reached the church. As for me, I know that a bride should be late for her own wedding—but not forty minutes! My driver managed to take the wrong road. Still, at last we arrived in Hastings, and were approaching the church. We were signalled to the west door, where Tom Savins was waiting, along with a full choir in red cassocks and white surplices.

I looked round for Cousin Rosamanda, who was my Maid-of-Honour, but I couldn't see her. She had gone to the usual entrance instead of to the west door, which was opened only on special occasions. (Mother Rutherford later told me that it reminded her of her own wedding at St Michael's Church, Beaconsfield, Buckinghamshire. She and Father Stringer *left* by the wrong door, and her friend Grace Bridges got showered with rice and confetti instead of them!)

The choir led the hymns. As we sang 'Lead Us Heavenly Father, lead us, / O'er the world's tempestuous sea' I remember thinking, 'It can't be more tempestuous than it has been already.'

Here was I, who had watched my sister, my many cousins and friends getting married, believing that I would never have a wedding of my own, trapped as I had been in a false identity; here was I, going to God's altar at last to marry the man of my choice. . . . But then our family motto is 'Nothing is impossible with

God.' It had certainly been an appropriate motto in my case.

There was a grand congregation of relatives and friends, plus sixteen photographers and television cameramen hidden discreetly behind the choir-stools in the chancel.

As we knelt on the marble chancel steps to be blessed, and the choir sang Joseph Barnaby's 'O Perfect Love', Mother Rutherford was so filled with emotion that she suddenly turned to everybody in church and said in a loud voice, *'Oh, isn't it wonderful!'*

It wasn't until a year later, while I was having lunch with the Reverend Savins and his wife, Margaret, that he said, 'You know when I was blessing you, I looked down and saw John-Paul's cowboy boots. All I could think of was Nancy Sinatra singing, 'These boots are meant for walking!'

CHAPTER FIVE

The reception following the ceremony was held in the Alexandra Hotel, which overlooks the sea. John-Paul's eyes kept straying to the window, and it was obvious to all how much he loved the water.

Mother Rutherford had broken her hip while filming in Italy, and was obliged to sit during the reception. But I think she enjoyed toasting us with champagne. The wedding cake had hard icing because she had heard that American cakes often have the soft kind. She wanted John-Paul to taste a real English wedding cake.

Friends and relations had come from many miles for the ceremony. The person they had known as Gordon was now Dawn, yet nobody embarrassed me with a stupid or thoughtless remark.

Suddenly I thought of all the turmoil back in Charleston and, flying in the face of etiquette, I decided to make a speech there and then. I began, 'You are looking at a brave man,' and I referred to John-Paul.

It was dark by time the reception was over. Some of us then returned to Cousin Rosamanda's, where we danced and drank more champagne. We then drove back to our London hotel, but managed to find a fish and chip shop on the drive so that John-Paul should savour the British way of eating this favourite dish. I was horrified to find the parcels were no longer wrapped in newspaper.

* * *

We spent our honeymoon at Elm Close, the Rutherford-Davis home at Gerrards Cross, Buckinghamshire. There, next day, Father Stringer cooked the after-wedding luncheon which he said was specially for John-Paul . . . roast beef, Yorkshire pudding and brussels sprouts. It was served on the exquisite family Rockingham china.

After lunch John-Paul went walking in the garden with Father Stringer, while I sat talking at the table with dear Mother Rutherford. 'Oh, they do like each other, don't they?' she said at least three times. 'Oh, I do want them to like each other.'

Then John-Paul came in carrying a single red rose which he presented to me.

'I've been teaching John-Paul how to be a background husband,' my Father Stringer said.

Elm Close stood well back from the main road in a little wooded glen. It was the home they had always wanted —'our final home,' Father Stringer used to call it. (They had previously lived in a small villa that Mother Rutherford had always referred to as 'the doll's house'.) At Elm Close they used to feed the countless birds that seemed to be always waiting in the trees and bushes at the front and in the two cedars at the rear. Indoors the chief meeting-place was the large sitting-room with its ingle-nook and mantelpiece from which 'Oscar' reigned supreme. Mother Rutherford had won her Academy Award statuette as Best Supporting Actress for her performance in *The V.I.P.'s*, with Elizabeth Taylor and Richard Burton. The fire never seemed to go out, even during the night, while a peaceful feeling of home and security encompassed us. It was the happiest time of my life with John-Paul, for he really felt an affinity with my adoptive parents, as they did with him. Once he even washed the dishes, something he never did for me!

For a brief spell the storms of Charleston were forgotten. We listened to music, Mother Rutherford read to us, we sang, laughed and were truly a family. I hated to think that all too soon it would end.

Of John-Paul Father Stringer told me privately, 'He would be a gentleman in any society.'

The social hours we kept at Elm Close were dictated by Mother Rutherford's little periods of rest. At 4 p.m. Father Stringer served tea with little iced cakes, and everybody chatted. Mother Rutherford always called Father Stringer 'Dear Heart'. Father Stringer then played to us upon the piano, including some of his own compositions. This greatly impressed John-Paul! At 10 p.m. we were all summoned to the kitchen for eggs and bacon, which was a nightly tradition at Elm Close. Mother Rutherford presided, wearing a thick green wool dressing-gown and hair net. It seemed so strange to be able to sit there with the window curtains undrawn. There was nothing to be afraid of.

When the time came for us to leave them we set off down the drive, past the old-fashioned street light, and turned back for a last wave. There they both stood, she in her hair net and robe, the latter now augmented by one of the famous green capes which, following her death, we gave to the Victoria and Albert Museum in London.

I asked John-Paul what he had liked best of all at Elm Close. He replied, 'The Oscar!'

* * *

Back in London we settled into our hotel. Then John-Paul thought he would like to take a walk. Three hours later he had still not returned. I was very worried, and then he telephoned. He asked me to come at once and to bring seven hundred pounds. I asked him where he was, and he gave the address of a nightclub in Soho.

I went downstairs and asked for the night manager, who said it was a terrible dive and that he would call Scotland Yard to help me rescue my husband.

There was I in a nightgown under my mink, driving off to Soho in a police car with two detectives and two policemen. I had never met anybody from Scotland Yard before, so in spite of the circumstances it was rather exciting.

The night club was in a basement, so we had to descend a flight of steps. Finally we came face to face with the manager who was demanding his money. I asked John-Paul what on earth he had ordered to run up such a huge bill. He replied that everybody was suddenly drinking champagne, and he didn't realize that he was paying for it.

After a big argument the detectives got us out of the place in one piece, and told John-Paul it was a wonder he hadn't been found next morning with a knife in his back.

We didn't have to pay the bill, though. And at least I got to have a ride in a police car!

On the flight back to America there was one small, but annoying incident. Since my husband wasn't able to read, I usually ordered from the menu for both of us. I said to the airline hostess, who was from Georgia, 'And my husband would like . . .' The jackass, looking at a white man in the seat opposite, replied: 'Is that your husband over there?'

We arrived back at our home on Society Street, there to find that Miss Nelly, one of the two chihuahuas that had travelled with me all over the world, and had substituted for children in my old, barren life, had died. Knowing how much I had loved Miss Nelly, John-Paul dug up her little body, dressed it in a little blue coat that she had worn in life, and reburied her in my jewel-box.

CHAPTER SIX

A friend heard the following remark by a fellow guest at a dinner-party he attended in Charleston: 'The only way to get her Black husband to leave her is to put her on the street.' The words were spoken by a representative of a savings and loan association—the very association, as it happened, that would put the threat into action.

Following the death in 1962 of my cousin, Isabel Lydia Whitney, I had bought—as I have described—a derelict mansion, of historic interest, in the district of Ansonborough, now one of the most fashionable and expensive sections of real estate in Charleston, but then a run-down slum.

I had sunk about $220,000 into the restoration of the big house. V. Sackville-West, the author and famous gardener, had written from Sissinghurst Castle in England to advise me on the garden plans. Shrubbery had been brought from all parts of the world. Inside, the house was furnished with my own collection of antiques and paintings augmented by those I had inherited from Cousin Isabel.

The late S. Henry Edmunds, husband of the Director of Historic Charleston Foundation, from whom I purchased the house, had arranged for a loan from a savings and loan association in Charleston, and this I had extended so as to provide a suitable gallery for my cousin's paintings over what had been the old kitchen.

Until my engagement to John-Paul Simmons, the house had been a featured part of the annual spring tours arranged by the Historic Charleston Foundation, who even supplied a guard for the collection of antiques. Suddenly, upon my engagement, all this was stopped.

A year or so after my marriage I was amused to be told, by a young man whose grandmother was a local leader of society, that she had said the reason why my house was removed from their tours was because I had too many naked Adonises on display inside! As I have never been fond of nude paintings and sculpture, this statement is incomprehensible! There wasn't one piece of naked 'Adonis' art in the mansion. If they were referring to John-Paul, even I didn't see what he looked like undressed until after I had married him, and then not for several weeks, for he always undressed in the dark.

My immediate neighbours were always friendly. One, the respected Mamie Cobb, often described how John-Paul had saved her life when a group of men were about to attack her. A young White nurse in the apartment house next door told a similar story; that he had come to her rescue in a similar situation.

There were, however, a group of individuals who decided that in marrying Black I was now Black, and that their property values would henceforth decrease. The same group was vociferous in trying to prevent a group of Black teaching nuns from moving to a new convent close by. (It's not that we don't like nuns,' insisted one faded belle noted for her 'culture', 'we just like old houses'.) The tactics employed against us were a combination of physical and mental harassment.

First the insurances on the house were suddenly called in by a Broad Street insurance agent who declared the house a storm risk, even though it was constructed like a castle with walls several feet thick. Another leading insurance man, when asked to take up the insurance, said, 'What are you trying to do to me?'

In the end, James Arthur Williams, the antique authority from Savannah, Georgia, insured the property for me by threatening to withdraw his own insurances from a Savannah company if they did not immediately issue a policy on 56, Society Street.

This insurance crisis was hanging over us all one Christmas, when both of us were half dead from Hong Kong flu. Jim Williams proved the best Santa Claus I ever knew, for, if the house was uninsured, the savings and loan association could have forced an immediate sale of the property. Ironically enough, the president of this savings and loan association and his wife had often been guests in my home!

It has amazed friends in other parts of the United States (and, in fairness, many friends in the South), and relatives abroad, that in a city where preservation is supposed to be of primary importance, the systematic destruction of 56, Society Street could be allowed with scarcely one voice raised to stop it. Is Christian marriage such a crime?

I will confess that at times I was so weary that the only solace I knew was in bed . . . where I lay hoping that I would not wake up next morning. I am supposed to forgive those responsible. I try, but even now the sinking sense of despair and sheer horror lingers. When one woman, who had taken me for some $1,500 with a false lien against my property, died, John-Paul remarked: 'Well, all she got was enough to bury her!'

There simply was no rest, for telephone calls came in through each and every night from mysterious females who claimed they were sleeping with my husband in some motel. Often he was in bed beside me when they called. It was all part of a campaign to wear down my resistance and stir up confusion in my home. But Operation Telephone failed to work.

Far more wearying and frightening were the petty officials who invaded our privacy in response to complaints from the racist oppressors who wished us to move. I opened the front door one morning to be knocked down by at least a dozen men, who charged in, doubling up on top of one another concertina fashion as in an early Mack Sennett comedy. They were representatives of the health department, building department and fire department. There was a lone Black among them, whom John-Paul called 'a disgrace to his race', carrying a notebook in which to make 'observations'.

The fire department officer seemed very disgruntled and upset. He took one look at the electrical wiring system—which had cost me thousands of dollars—and grumbled, 'I can't condemn this wiring. It's better than what we've got at the fire station.' He did, however, demand that a car standing in the driveway be removed . . . it was apparently a fire hazard. I couldn't see why, as John-Paul had gutted it and was making it into an armoured car for me. Besides, the old lady next door had for years kept a vintage car standing in her yard. She refused to sell it because it had been her late husband's.

John-Paul hadn't exactly helped the overall situation by presenting me with a baby pig, called Frances. She came from John's Island. James, the butler, did not see eye to eye with me on Frances' diet. However, I had my way, and, even though fed like an English pig, she prospered. Frances could not be kept in the city and eventually went off to Wadmalaw Island where she married another pet pig named Bono. Before she left, however, Frances unexpectedly encountered a lady realtor who was looking over the house. I don't know who showed the most surprise, the lady or Frances! I do know that only the lady screamed.

Following our return from England we had received a large crate of wedding presents from my relatives and friends. These had been shipped from London and had arrived in Charleston in record time. The crate was delivered to our house late one wintry afternoon and deposited in the driveway. It was such a large box, the size of a small room, that I suggested to John-Paul we open it next day, for dismantling it looked like a major task. He disagreed, saying that we should do the job immediately. As it turned out, he was right.

The presents were brought safely indoors, but the crate, filled with straw and wrapping papers, was left next to the big, iron entrance gates. In the early hours of the morning, Jackie, my faithful German Shepherd, and Banji the Ubangi, started to bark. Awakened by the noise, I gradually became aware of a roaring, hissing sound. I shook John-Paul and he leapt out of bed. Thrusting his head out of the window, he shouted, 'Good God, the bastards have set us on fire!'

Had it not been for Jackie and Banji, and the prompt arrival of the firetruck, we must have burned in our beds. As it was, much of the driveway foliage was damaged. The porches were scorched and, had the fire gone undetected, not only our house would have gone up in smoke but probably our next-door neighbours.

As soon as we were rescued I went over to a friendly neighbour, Robert Holmes on Anson Street, and telephoned the F.B.I. As a result, I was instructed not to disturb the charred debris of the crate until an arson expert had seen it. John-Paul had already discovered the cause of the fire—a home-made firebomb made with a Coca-Cola bottle, which had been tossed into the crate by a nameless enemy.

The following afternoon a policeman called and said that if we didn't remove the debris at once (the firemen had pulled it out to the curb), he would give me a ticket! I couldn't believe my ears, and even when I told him of my instructions from the F.B.I. he totally disregarded me.

Next day, Robert P. Stockton, a reporter with the Charleston *News and Courier*, told me that while he was on duty manning the city desk that afternoon a man called three times to say I was blocking the sidewalk, and demanding that something be done about it. According to Mr Stockton, the anonymous caller did not have a Southern accent.

I don't know which was worse, the mental harassment or the physical violence.

John Paul was shot at in the street . . . a man tried to run him and his dog down with a car. I was set upon and knocked on to a concrete sidewalk by a white man who earlier had baited me with the words, 'Nigger lover,' every time he passed in his car. He was chiefly incensed that I took no notice. He broke my left shoulder. John-Paul thought that I fell while dusting the top of the refrigerator. I dared not tell him the truth for, with his fierce temper, he might well have killed the attacker.

The fear of a sniper's bullet was always with us. When our engagement was announced we had walked up Charleston's main thoroughfare, King Street, where the curious crowded the store windows to watch us. One needed iron nerves. On that particular evening we came home to hear that Robert Kennedy had been shot. Even while mourning him, it brought home to us the precariousness of our own situation.

I was so often spat upon that it became a commonplace. I got to know just when somebody was going to whisper my identity to her companion, who would then turn and stare. One particular Episcopal minister's wife, who would be better employed visiting the poor and needy—of which the city has plenty—instead of shopping for antiques, was a prime offender.

I knew that sometime I would lose my calm and stick out my tongue! But, as the proverb has it, 'Sticks and stones may break my bones, but names can never hurt me . . .'

CHAPTER SEVEN

When I was a child there was a furore in our family because a cousin got herself 'into trouble' and had to get married. George Ditch, my favourite uncle, cursed and said, 'They had a bloody old sing-song in Heathfield Church today.' My aunt declared: 'It's as though I had a priceless figurine which fell and broke into a thousand pieces.'

I understood their disappointment, however, when the husband I adored crashed without warning from the pedestal upon which I had placed him. I was in bed with John-Paul when he suddenly confessed that he was the father of a baby boy. The child had been conceived before our marriage and was born some months afterwards.

For the moment I was stunned, but I did not lose my head, nor say anything for which I might later have been sorry. I was still European enough to realize that men do stray, yet expect their wives to remain completely faithful. Before we were married John-Paul had remarked, 'Gentlemen mess with whores but marry ladies.' I'd jotted the phrase down, thinking what a good theme for a book it would make.

My first thought was for the child. I have always loved children. At first John-Paul told me only that the mother was a young, innocent girl who admired me very much and didn't want to hurt me. I think he exaggerated a little. When I asked if there was any chance of our adopting the child and giving him his proper place and name, my husband shook his head. One night, however, he rushed in with something wrapped in a hospital towel. He tripped and dropped 'it' on the bed. For the moment I thought he had brought me another puppy, but it was a baby. John-Paul had obviously been drinking, for he promptly fell asleep. I guessed it was his child and I took the best care I could of the little mite. Fortunately, I had a feeding bottle handy. Next morning I was awakened by some children shouting in the street: 'They have our baby inside.' I woke John-Paul, who took the child back to its mother. My mother-in-law said that I must sink my pride, that I was Mrs Simmons and that Charleston was full of 'old heifers' who took other women's husbands.

The shock of learning about John-Paul's baby was softened when I found that we were to have one of our own. For some weeks I lived in bliss. Everything would be all right now, I thought.

Then Margie, my darling mother, died very suddenly. I discovered the fact when a letter of sympathy arrived out of the blue from England. I fell on the floor with shock, suffering a miscarriage. For days I was so crazed I believed that the child had been safely born.

Realization gradually dawned upon me, but the empty pain did not go away. I hated to pass mothers walking out with their babies on the street. I wanted a child so much.

Cruellest of all was that my mother-in-law kept a picture of John-Paul's baby displayed on top of the television that I had given her. I had never hated or resented the baby . . . but how could anybody do that? I desperately resented the constant reminder that I had on child of my own.

At the time of our engagement John-Paul had told a New York news cameraman that he would like three children: 'One black . . . one white . . . and a little Vietnamese baby for good measure.' I had heard how difficult it was to adopt Vietnamese babies conceived by American fathers, so as I had connections in Korea, a country about which I had written, I thought that adoption might be possible there. Long negotiations were made through the Korean Ambassador in London, but these ended abruptly when the orphanage discovered we were not Catholics. So that dream was ended. This was our only attempt to adopt a child. In any case, adoption requests from America would be referred to local South Carolinian agencies for an investigation of the prospective parents' circumstances. Not in a thousand years would they have allowed a mixed couple, who had contracted such a controversial marriage, to adopt any child.

John-Paul never neglected his son. The child was given everything, and more, that he needed. I used to call him 'the little Prince'.

I was pleasantly surprised by all the sympathy I received from friendly Blacks over John-Paul's baby. But their vindictiveness towards the innocent child itself completely stunned me. 'Leave it on the street' was a refrain repeated so often by so-called Christian church-goers, it made me sick. One man made it his business to stop me on Market Street to say that he was the father of the child, and not my husband.

Prayer helped a great deal. My Catholic great-grandmother, Marta Hall, had brought with her from the Seville convent where she was raised an old wood and gesso statue of St Teresa of Avila, patron saint of writers. Over the years this statue has been of much comfort to me. I stood it on the table that served as altar at my Charleston marriage. I tell St Teresa everything, and I feel she helped bring me safely through a very difficult situation. I had accepted what had happened for I still loved my husband. At least he had been honest enough to tell me. Unlike many men who fathered children out of wedlock, he had not shirked his responsibilities. I admired him for that.

CHAPTER EIGHT

I never told my adoptive parents about the baby. They held John-Paul in such esteem. I could not bear to shatter their illusions about him, for they were so proud of our marriage.

Father Stringer wrote to me to say they had received an uninvited female visitor from high society Charleston, who made the train journey from London to Gerrards Cross especially to berate us. Father Stringer and Mother Rutherford apparently received this stranger on the doorstep of Elm Close, where, after speaking her piece, she received a good 'telling off' from both of them. Once again, Father Stringer reminded me that John-Paul would be a gentleman in any society. It is typical of Mother Rutherford and Father Stringer that he could go on to say:

> After we felt we had thoroughly made our point about you both and that we didn't believe a word she had said, we thought that we had better behave like civilized human beings and ask her in. She drank three cups of tea and ate a whole plate of cucumber sandwiches and three cream puffs.

Meantime, in Charleston we lived from day to day. Some nice people chose personal kindness rather than downright cruelty. But they were sadly in a minority.

Among the faithful was a civilized New York expatriate, Robert Holmes, who lived just round the corner. He was a connoisseur of the arts, and we shared mutual friends in the world of art in which I had once moved with my cousin, Isabel Whitney. It was always a joy to escape from my troubles by visiting Robert and talking to him of books, paintings and French period furniture.

Opposite us lived Mrs Mamie Cobb, who rented apartments. 'Miss Mamie' worked harder than any person I ever knew. She was fiercely loyal, and following the incident I mentioned in which John-Paul saved her life from a gang of hooligans she said she felt safe just knowing that he lived close by. One of her tenants, Tommy Cantwell, who came from a respected local family of Irish descent, was also very kind to me. As times got harder for me he would always, when he got his veteran's disability cheque, ask me if I needed a dollar or two.

In the end I put the mansion on the market so that we might move to a more friendly neighbourhood. Among the realtors who tried to sell it was a lady of uncertain age who announced with much confidence, 'After I've sold your house I can have my face lifted!' Unfortunately, she and her face had reckoned without the combined efforts of Miss Jackie, our German Shepherd, Banji the Ubangi, Rutherford-Davis the chihuahua, and Rupert-Ranger, the bull terrier. They had all taken a distinct dislike to the face she already had. The last straw came when John-Paul brought home a large black German Shepherd, whom I named Peter. One day, while the lady realtor was showing a client round the house, Peter suddenly leapt clear over her head. She nearly had a heart-attack, and the client wasn't exactly amused.

A night or two later I was walking on Anson Street

when the realtor shot past in her car. She braked suddenly, poked her head through the window and shouted, 'What are you trying to do to me?' I was utterly mystified. Then, upon turning the corner, I heard the dogs barking frantically and saw Tommy Cantwell leaning out of his window. 'I've called the police,' he yelled. 'There was a mad woman shaking your gates and screaming, "If it wasn't for your dogs I could have had my face lifted." '

Not long afterwards I was visiting Miss Mamie when she told me she had cancer. She fought bravely, and actually seemed to have the disease licked. But during her convalescence she succumbed to a massive heart-attack. It was the end for Tommy also. He went steadily downhill. Late one afternoon I saw a crowd gathered by Miss Mamie's house, and an ambulance. Tommy was a middle-aged bachelor and had nobody to accompany him to hospital, so I jumped up into the ambulance and held his hand. 'Thank you for all you have done for me,' he whispered.

Mr Tommy Cantwell died quietly in the Emergency Room. It was a rare privilege to have served him at the last, and I know it would have pleased Miss Mamie, who had been so nice to us, that I had been able to help.

The late Henry Edmunds, my lawyer, used to say that given a fair chance I would always make money. I had come to America at the age of nineteen with two dollars in my pocket. How was I able to buy the mansion?

It had been financed in the main with the proceeds of a successful book, *Golden Boats from Burma*, which had been a Book Club selection, and I earned about forty thousand dollars from a book about my early life.

Cousin Isabel had also left me money, most of which had gone into restoring the fabric of the mansion. She had also left me some furniture, which I brought to Charleston. Everything else I made through feature articles, and through buying and selling paintings and antiques, about which I knew a good deal. For although we had been poor when I was a child, I had a number of very rich relations, some of whom taught me to recognize a good piece of antique furniture. At about ten years of age I bought my first antique, a china cabinet, with money I had carefully saved from prizes won in the children's section of the local horticultural show. I had also bred rabbits and sold them. My first bicycle was purchased from thirty shillings earned for looking after a lady's hot house while she was on holiday.

Thus I can honestly say that the house on Society Street, bought before I was thirty, was the result of a tradition of hard work. People have asked, 'Where did all that money go?'

Most of it went to save the house from the wolves who were gnawing at the door. Thousands of dollars just disappeared. John-Paul had a heart bigger than his pocket, and I admit that I tend to think with my heart rather than my head. My husband had a passion for cars, especially Thunderbirds. He had three! One of them he decided to turn into an armoured car for my protection. He first covered it with chicken wire and then poured cement over the top. I never did have a ride, for it collapsed under the weight! (The vehicle that towed it away capped the whole episode when it knocked down one of the gate pillars.)

He also had three boats. One was bought from an old

fisherman. When I went to inspect our purchase I couldn't find my husband. The old fisherman, dead drunk, was wearing a brand new suit, which I suspected I had paid for. He mumbled on about going to the country to get special lumber to repair the prow of something that closely resembled a Noah's Ark. As far as I know it never saw the ocean, and today it lies abandoned and rotting on the banks of Mosquito Creek.

Another boat that John-Paul bought lay miles away from the water in somebody's backyard. It's probably still there.

The third boat cost twenty-five hundred dollars, plus a thousand more for fitting it with a new bottom.

A thousand dollars disappeared from a secret drawer in my desk, and at the same time a certain lady's house had two rooms of new furniture, including fine marble-topped tables.

In a fit of generosity he bought his mother nearly two thousand dollars' worth of furniture, including a grandfather clock. I was asked to inspect it and found myself making the down payment and responsible for several hundred dollars monthly in payments. One blistering summer's day I walked the streets trying to sell a painting to pay the instalment due. When I came home, John-Paul was lying on an Aubusson carpet in the drawing-room playing a trumpet! That was when I gave up trying to meet the instalments. The furniture company retaliated by taking a magnificent bed that John-Paul had bought me . . . not his mother's. I had spent thousands in cash with that store. The sheriff's deputy added insult to injury by asking if I had any religious pictures to sell!

John-Paul was very upset when they took our bed, and blaming me he said: 'I hope you're satisfied now.'

As for cars, they needed more repairs than any cars my British relatives ever had. My old butler kept telling me where the money was going, but love can be blind. My husband boasted that he had given his son enough money to see him through to Social Security. Priceless miniatures vanished from the wall, and valuable furnishings disappeared. One 'friend' told another, 'Don't you ever bring Dawn to my home without giving me warning. I have to put things away first!'

I have to admit that the group of White racists who were out to get me for bringing a Black husband into their neighbourhood were being aided and abetted, however unwittingly, by someone much nearer home.

The tragedy of it all, and many intelligent Blacks have told me they know it, is that here was an opportunity to continue the management of the Society Street mansion as a house museum . . . the only one in the city belonging to and operated by a Black family. By destroying it, future generations of Blacks, our own daughter included, have been robbed and cheated.

But I have always believed that my husband was being taken advantage of. I still do. In the beginning my under-butler, Gussie Lewis, came to me and said that 'a certain lady' had admitted to him: 'I can't stand that old stink-ass John-Paul, but I'm going to get some of that money . . . and if I had a son old enough I would send him to look after Dawn . . . and get it both ways.'

I felt sick when he told me, and could only say, 'What kind of a woman is this?'

CHAPTER NINE

The British rights to my autobiography, called *Man Into Woman*, were actually sold during our wedding reception in Hastings. Mother Rutherford said this was quite in order, and that some of her most important acting contracts had been made 'over the garden fence'.

Patrick Jenkins, editor with the publishers and a close friend of Mother Rutherford and Father Stringer, was at the wedding. I believe I was eating a piece of my own wedding cake when he gave me the good news.

But publication was delayed for various reasons over a period of some fifteen months. I kept expecting the call to England to launch the book. On 23 June 1970 Mother Rutherford wrote from Elm Close:

Patrick will soon be letting you know about the book. He thinks very well of it. And now till your stay here approaches, our love, Dear.

However, it was not until March 1971 that I actually left for England. I set out alone. My husband volunteered to stay and look after the house. We dared not leave it unguarded.

The night before my departure John-Paul and his black German Shepherd Peter were nearly run down in the street by a car driven at them by a White male. Peter was badly hurt, so my departure next day was a sad one. I was weary both physically and mentally when I got on the plane.

I arrived at London Airport to be met by Patrick Jenkins who gave me the news that I was to be interviewed by Molly Parkin for *The Sunday Times* at breakfast. I felt such a mess, even though I was wearing a beautiful mink coat that Ritchia Atkinson, a friend of mine from Louisiana, had given me on a visit to Charleston. We were lunching one day and she decided it would give my morale a boost if we exchanged coats. Mine was made of cloth!

Miss Parkin was a most elegantly dressed young lady. She wore a purple maxi-coat, a 'Paper Moon' over-the-ears beret, and carried a purple shoulder bag. She said that it amazed her how relaxed I was after the long journey. I hope she didn't realize what an effort it took for me to control my nerves. All I longed for was to be in bed! Her article was excellent, very observant and penetrating. It was the first time that anybody had ever called me an introvert, which I really am. I will always endeavour to be friendly and a success in public, if it is expected of me, but I am happiest living my own private life within the four walls of my home. She wrote:

The last third of the book makes in many ways the most interesting reading. Gordon has become Dawn, the name decided upon by John-Paul Simmons, the young negro fisherman she has married. It is a grippingly convincing love story which appears to have survived obstacles which separately would not seem problems.

She is rich, he is poor. She is an intellectual and introvert. He is a boisterous exuberant extrovert. He lives by his body, she by her mind. He is young, she is almost ten years his senior. He is a healthy hetero-sexual, she until their marriage had been sexually totally inexperienced. The wish even to kiss had not been there. She lived alone, but for her servants, in one of Charleston's most famous and historic houses. He lived, hurly-burly, one of eleven happy children, with his mother and father in a different street alto-gether in Charleston. And yet for both it was a case of love at first sight.

Living as they did, and still do, in South Carolina, the question of their colour was explosive. Their wedding was front-page news and they became the target for racial malcontents throughout America. They have suffered incredible victimisation and literally, in Charleston, walk in fear of their lives. Both have been physically attacked, their pets have been poisoned, and they are pestered continuously by bomb scares, threatening letters and menacing phone calls.

It is obvious that for their own safety they should move from Charleston, but they have steadfastly re-sisted. Their courage and tenacity and certainly their love survives the ordeals. We leave the story with them surviving a further grief. Dawn's mother dies. She gets word casually, too late to attend the funeral of the woman she had always idolised.

The severe shock causes Dawn's miscarriage. The electrifying glorious fact of her pregnancy has just been revealed to us almost as casually as her mother's death was to her.

After breakfast which included my favourite kippers, something I do not get in America, Patrick showed me a piece from Charles Greville's column in the *Daily Mail*. It read:

> Dame Margaret Rutherford will today be reunited with her adopted child, Dawn Langley Simmons. And the two have a lot to talk about. Not only has Dame Margaret's American-based author protégé changed sex, but also married a black fisherman. Mrs Simmons is in this country for the publication next week of her book *Man Into Woman*.

A very nice young lady turned up from the London *Evening News* to interview me for the John London column. She brought along a photographer who took rather a nice photograph. I looked very much like Margie and that always pleases me. She wrote:

> Dawn Langley Simmons describes herself as an old-fashioned woman married to an old-fashioned man.
> 'Who else today has the sort of husband who will go out and bring you back armfuls of fresh wild flowers?' she asked.

On arrival at Elm Close, I was grieved to see just how much Mother Rutherford had failed since the wedding. She now walked with two sticks, that brave, dear soul whose vigorous steps had carried her through so many plays and films. Father Stringer waited upon her hand and foot. She could not bear him to be out of her sight. Even when he took a few minutes off to shave she was calling, 'Dear Heart, dear Heart, where are you?' With all the strain he had aged terribly.

As I give thanks for my happiest, peaceful week spent with John-Paul at our English wedding, so am I equally grateful for those last dear days at Elm Close with my adoptive parents. The time for pretending was over, their little world was crumbling around them.

The weather was quite frosty and one morning the garden at Elm Close was covered with a sprinkling of snow. This did not deter Mother Rutherford, frail as she was, from taking breakfast in the garden. I wore my mink coat and a long yellow muffler borrowed from Father Stringer, while Mother Rutherford, now somewhat shrunken, was dressed in green cape and pixie cap.

We drank coffee while Father Stringer threw crumbs to the birds, naming each variety just as he had done for Mother Rutherford when they were courting. There was even a fairy ring of snowdrops in the glen.

How timeless and right it all seemed. Somewhat selfishly, I wished it might go on forever. Then my thoughts turned to John-Paul and I knew that I had to go back to that tortured life in Charleston. The priest at Hastings had made us one flesh and extolled us to 'leave to one another'.

Every minute was precious to me. One Sunday afternoon, while they were resting, I took a little walk past the holly hedges and into the village. I had a wonderful time choosing all the favourite chocolate bars that we had enjoyed as children. In one shop I found two tiny furry toy rabbits, about an inch long. I gave one to Mother Rutherford, who always loved that sort of thing. The other is in my china cabinet.

Returning to the house I found that they were still asleep. Sinking into a comfortable armchair in the inglenook, I just stared into the fire. My only companion was Mother Rutherford's Oscar on the mantelpiece.

When they woke up Father Stringer prepared tea.

73

This was a ritual he loved, always shopping for the little fancy cakes himself. His buttered scones were delicious. Mother Rutherford poured the tea from a silver teapot. I tried not to notice how shaky she was. After tea Father Stringer played the piano, just as he had done for John-Paul. It made me feel very close to my dear one, then so far away.

For the party given to launch my book, Father Stringer chose my dress himself. It was a peacock-feather blue, with little gold metal rings around the waist. The pattern of the material gave it a sort of paisley effect. We set off for London in a car driven by Mrs Jones, the lady chauffeur who had driven us all in happier times. I remember she was wearing a jaunty peaked cap that made her look like a naval officer. The party was given in a large hotel—two porters carried Mother Rutherford up the front steps in a chair. It was a jolly affair. The press took family photographs of us together, and there was lots of champagne and plenty to eat.

Back at Elm Close that evening Mother Rutherford and I sat in the inglenook by the fire, while Father Stringer prepared rump steak and onions for supper. She picked up a book of poems and showed me the cover. They were written by Mary Wilson, wife of Prime Minister Harold Wilson. 'Let me read my favourite,' she said.

> IF I must die, as die I must
> First let me fully live,
> And grasp and hold a thousand joys,
> And take as well as give.

And let me no experience miss,
But taste and savour all,
And dance throughout the dazzling day
On which the dark will fall.

And may the pattern of my life
Lie strand on scarlet strand
'Til God leans from His sapphire throne—
The hour-glass in His hand.

Her voice, no longer strong, was still beautiful. I felt so privileged that this lovely woman whose acting ability had enchanted the world, should be reading just for me.

The next day I went by train to Eastbourne in Sussex, where I had spent many happy times as a child. I was going to stay with a friend of long standing, Nancy O. Basey, an Australian. Nancy O. had for many years been the companion of her aunt, Miss Helena Hall, an historian and author of several books, including a dictionary of the Sussex dialect which she had published at the age of eighty-six. Miss Hall had died some years earlier, and Nancy O. lived on in the dear little Georgian house called 'Blue Gate', overlooking the village green at Lindfield. When I spent my summers with Margie at Beecholme, Miss Hall and Nancy O., a very fast driver, would take us for forays into the English countryside. There had also been visits to 'Blue Gate', where Miss Helena dispensed treacle pudding and provided home-made dandelion wine, which we sipped from long-stemmed glasses under an apple tree in the garden. The ashes of her brother Jack had been scattered there.

Nancy O. had later given up the house and moved away. She was now on holiday in Sussex, staying at a little hotel in which she engaged a room for me.

We hired a car, and our first journey was to Sissinghurst to see Margie's grave. I had visited it with John-Paul at the time we were married, but now I particularly wanted to see the cross of grey Cornish granite, which I had ordered and paid for with part of the advance on my autobiography. My cousin John Ticehurst had designed and executed the memorial.

The cemetery, which lies behind Holy Trinity Church with a lovely view across the Kentish weald, is a peaceful spot. It is beautifully kept and we were well pleased with the stone. The epitaph that I had chosen was taken from the Bible:

SHE HATH DONE WHAT SHE COULD.

Little clumps of purple crocuses, planted by my sister Fay, were in full bloom. We filled a vase with daffodils, jonquils and mimosa.

I had never seen a primrose since I left England as a teenager. My visits home were always made during summer, after the primroses had bloomed. Now, as we left the grave, I noticed a primrose in full bloom. It seemed like a sign of hope.

Next we drove down to Sissinghurst Castle, home of the late V. Sackville-West and Harold Nicolson, who had encouraged me to write when I was a child, and then back to the village to visit Jack Copper, my natural father, then living out his widowerhood in Verdun Cottage.

He had a good fire awaiting us and had soon made

a pot of tea. His dog, Billy, had once belonged to Sir Harold. It covered us with white hairs!

Jack was on crutches, a tragic sight when one recalled the vigour and manliness that once had been his. Like my John-Paul, he had been a garage mechanic when Margie first met him and, as with John Paul, it had also been love at first sight for them. I had understood their turbulent love much better since my own hectic marriage. After Margie died very suddenly Jack seemed to give up, rather as Sir Harold, his employer, had done when the beloved Vita passed on. He lost the use of his legs, and was soon the ghost of his former self. Only the wit and caustic tongue remained. I was reminded of my Great-Aunt Jane Ticehurst who, in old age and sickness, cried: 'I may have shrunk but you'll still know me by the bite of my tongue.'

It was a moving visit to 'Poor Old Jack', as Nancy O. called him.

Next day we drove up to Marle Green to see Cousin Rosamanda. On the way I couldn't resist stopping at an antique shop. The owners must have seen fit to call the local newspaper, for when Nancy O., Rosamanda and I reached Heathfield Market we were immediately pursued by a press photographer. He seemed determined to photograph me buying a pair of hot pants! I am not the hot pants type, however, so he had to settle for something less exotic! The result was a photo and story in the *Sussex Express and County Herald*, extracts from which read:

Nostalgia took authoress Mrs Dawn Langley Simmons back to Heathfield Market on Tuesday to mingle, unrecognized, with the customers around the stalls.

Fur-coated Mrs Simmons, who was brought up in Old Heathfield, told a *Sussex Express* reporter: 'I used to be a regular visitor to the market and as a child used to breed rabbits and sell them at the market to get my pocket money. I always went to the furniture sales with my mother and of all the places I could have visited I felt I must come to the market. I have a soft spot for Heathfield.'

On leaving the market we drove to Tunbridge Wells, where Nancy O. left the car in the vicinity of the Pantiles. After lunch we returned to find we had a parking ticket. We were requested to go to the police station. This we did, and Nancy O., after saying that she was an Australian, declared: 'Well, I did ask a dustman if it was all right to park there!' Came the reply from the officer in charge: 'Next time, Madam, I suggest you ask a policeman.' With this admonition we were then to go on.

We had a quiet supper in the Dorset Arms, a fine old coaching inn near Withyham. There was a log fire in the hearth, and all was peace. I wished that John-Paul might be there, recalling the beautiful words describing the purpose of marriage in our Church of England wedding service: 'It was ordained for the mutual society, help, and comfort, that the one ought to have of the other, both in prosperity and adversity. . . .'

Next day we lunched at Hastings with the Reverend and Mrs Thomas G. Savins. Tom had blessed our marriage, and I returned to pray in St Clement's Church. There I was photographed by an *Evening Argus* photographer, as I signed the visitors' book, the Dante Gabriel Rossetti memorial as a background.

Back in London I went to see the Harley Street specialist who had been so helpful to Mother Rutherford and me by setting my medical facts right for posterity. He confirmed that another child was on the way.

I was so sure that it would be a little boy!

CHAPTER TEN

I returned home to chaos. Peter, John-Paul's black German Shepherd, had been so badly hurt in the accident beforeI left that he'd had to be put down. His loss had upset John-Paul very much, and it was clear that my husband was very mixed up.

The mortgage loan company joined hands with a number of people to put liens against the house. They made strange bedfellows. One woman who had not been paid conveniently forgot she had never given back an antique lamp and quilt belonging to me. One of these items was returned in the summer of 1973, over two years later.

The savings and loan association were $3,200 in arrears, a sum that could have been raised by the liquidation of one or two paintings in New York. However, they demanded repayment of the mortgage in full. There was no chance of getting the amount of money needed. Everybody ignored the fact that I had sunk $220,000 into the property which certainly had encouraged others to buy property into what was until then a rundown slum area. Today it is one of the most valuable parcels of real estate in the city of Charleston.

Losing the house made me think of how, as a small child with Margie, I had watched the bailiffs hammer up the windows of a house at Bailey's Hill, Sevenoaks, after putting a poor family out. The horror of this

Gordon during the early days, probably in Canada.

More perfectly atrocious pictures of me. The others
present include Philadelphia, Simon, Annabel and Nelly.

Above Near my home in Greenwich Village. *Below* Margaret Rutherford and me in New York, 1959.

Mother Rutherford and I discuss wedding finery.
Happier times.

Together with John-Paul.

The wedding at St. Clement's
Church, Hastings.

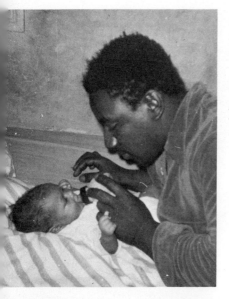

Above John-Paul and I televising in London prior to our Hastings wedding, 1969.

Left John-Paul and our joy, Natasha aged six weeks.

My favourite photograph (Natasha aged ten months).

incident had remained with me down the years. Now it was happening to me.

I have tried not to be bitter; but I feel that God will punish the guilty. Some have already been punished. When one of them died, John-Paul remarked: 'Just enough blood money to pay for the funeral.'

The Dr Joseph Johnson House, number 56, Society Street, home of Dawn Pepita and John-Paul Simmons, was sold on the steps of the courthouse as John-Paul's ancestors had been. The auction was spiced with dirty wisecracks from some of the attending 'gentlemen'.

Ritchia Atkinson came up from Louisiana to be with me. She gave me a new yellow dress and a wide-brimmed hat, then insisted that we have lunch at the King Charles Inn so that people might see me still proud and undefeated.

Joe Trott, the local florist, came across during our meal and said, 'How are you on your day of travail?'

'Fine, thank you,' I replied.

Nobody knew in Charleston that a child was coming. I had life in me; something else to live for.

Vincent Sottile, then deputy mayor of the city, represented me at the sale. I did have some good friends in high places. After it was over he told me: 'Now show everybody. Anybody can fall down but it takes a real person to get up again.'

Mr Sottile arranged for me to meet the new owners, Mr and Mrs Thomas Hutchinson. They had purchased the house for $42,500 from the sheriff. Quite a bargain.

I showed them around with as much dignity as a retiring First Lady in the White House, giving them photographs and important literature pertaining to the historic mansion.

81

Mr Sottile had told me that I would have seventeen days in which to vacate the property, and this seemed civilized. I said that I would like to remove the caskets containing the ashes of Annabel-Eliza and Miss Nelly, the twin chihuahuas who had accompanied me on my world travels; of Richard-Rufus, who had been to the White House and barked at President Lyndon B. Johnson; and of Josephine, John-Paul's beloved chihuahua and my Rutherford-Davis's mother. The Hutchinsons raised no objection to any of this.

After they had gone I felt better, as Mr Sottile was negotiating for our move into a house in another, friendlier section of town. I was horrified next morning to receive a registered letter from a woman lawyer ordering me to leave the property in twelve hours!

Of all the letters I have ever received in my life, this was by far the cruellest.

The possessions she generously said I might 'leave on the porch' included a pair of Sevres urns, the duplicates of which stand on the mantelpiece of the Blue Room in the White House. Mrs Lyndon B. Johnson pointed them out to me.

Mr Hutchinson blew out the votive light in front of my statue of St Teresa of Avila, patron saint of writers. It had been burning for nearly ten years without incident, but he was afraid it might set fire to 'his' house.

With John-Paul gone home to his Mama's, I left 56, Society Street accompanied by faithful Jackie, the German Shepherd; Banji the Ubangi, Rutherford-Davis, Lizzie Wormulus and Emily Louisa, the chihuahuas. Mr Hutchinson's mother-in-law was cutting down shrubbery as we closed the front door behind us.

I was Mrs John-Paul Simmons, Black by marriage;

the adopted daughter of Dame Margaret Rutherford, O.B.E., and the great-granddaughter of a Spanish condesa. Provincial revenge on me for my marriage failed to quench my pride.

The following Sunday John-Paul accompanied me back to 56, Society Street for the pets' ashes. It was perfectly horrible. Mr Hutchinson had just broken into Richard and Josephine's grave. We retrieved their scattered bones and Annabel-Eliza and Miss Nelly's caskets. Poor John-Paul; it had made him sick. I can only say that I was appalled at man's inhumanity to man.

I returned once more to arrange for an old car of John-Paul's to be towed away by a wrecker. Mr Hutchinson told me that in return I might take Simon the guinea-pig's tombstone. Poor Simon. We had to leave him behind. Mr Hutchinson did not honour his promise.

CHAPTER ELEVEN

We moved into an old house that had been empty for a long time. I paid the owners the sum of $2,500, as an option to buy. This was, I realize now, a very silly thing to do, but we were desperate and beggars can't be choosers.

I had to do all the packing myself. I found somebody to move me but couldn't find my husband, who was still with his Mama. I was hurt at the time but realized afterwards that with his quick temper, 56, Society Street was not the place for him. He kept remembering the desecration of Josephine's grave.

The new home was located at the corner of Thomas and Warren Streets, in a predominantly Black area. The lock had been stolen from the front door, while the back door never did shut properly. There were many broken windows and the mosquitoes that flew through in transit were terrible. I paid a contractor $200 to mend them and he disappeared with my money. The paint was peeling from the walls; it was dismal. The only thing that I liked was a chinaberry tree with its feathery purple flowers growing in the garden next door.

John-Paul seemed to give up entirely, and sold his $2,500 boat for $300. A new bottom had recently cost a thousand dollars. I don't know what he did with the money, although his Mama did make a point of telling me that he was seen sitting out with a certain lady and that they were both wearing brand new outfits.

I had developed a craving for turnips, and as I later told a friendly neighbour, 'If I was in the country I could always pull one out of a field.' Just to survive I used to walk down town every day to sell what was left of my jewellery and porcelains for a fraction of what they were worth. I know just how Scarlet O'Hara felt when she spoke those memorable words: 'I'll never be hungry again.'

Jackie, Banji, Rutherford, Lizzie Wormulus and Emily Louisa were with me. We all starved together.

Mother Rutherford and Father Stringer wanted us both to come 'home', and on 16 January 1971 wrote:

There will be a bedroom for you any time you like, if you are prepared to take pot-luck. We're rather invalidly and ramshackle.

With Mother Rutherford's continued disability they were likewise going through a very difficult period, yet they always had time for us. Father Stringer, as usual, was chief cook and bottle-washer. He was coping valiantly but to the detriment of his own health.

John-Paul disappeared for days at a time. He was subject to violent attacks similar to the one that he had the night of our engagement in New York City. Then, after a very happy day, in full view of everybody at the Prince George Hotel, he suddenly kicked me and hit my face hard enough to break an earring. Horrified, the Black porters ran for a first-aid kit; blood was pouring down my leg. When I went up to bed he was quite becalmed. He did not seem to know what had come over him.

One night I returned to find every picture-frame in the house smashed, and the albums I was preparing for

Duke University's Black History files slashed to pieces. There was blood everywhere, for John-Paul had cut himself badly in the process. Next evening he was back again, sitting on the doorstep with his possessions in a bundle. I did not say anything, and the next thing I knew he was in bed. Like most men, he believed all problems could be solved there.

I think we both suffered from reaction to the final, dreadful days at Society Street. Even now my heart beats faster when I see a group of men standing in front of my house. I think for one terrible moment that the goon squad, as we called the petty officials who harassed us, have returned.

One night Ritchia Atkinson, who lived near by, took me to a movie in her car, but had to leave in the middle of the film for a glass of water. She apparently took sick and did not return. I walked home, taking the Vanderhorst Street route, thinking I would be safe because I had to pass the police station. I wasn't.

I was followed by two men who attacked me as I turned on to Thomas Street. They tried to drag me into an empty house but I clung to the iron fence outside and screamed. I also bit one of them. God was with me, for a Black neighbour turned the corner from Warren Street in his car. He leapt out, pointed his gun at them and they ran off.

I went with a policeman and showed him the house where the men had been saying good night to a woman at the door. Nobody was ever caught. I received a long letter from Police Chief John F. Conroy in which he said that since I could not identify my attackers, nothing could be done. But I had gone with the policeman to the house where I had seen them, and a woman there said that one of them had been her brother! She even agreed with my description of what he was wearing. As a former newspaper reporter for such newspapers as the *Winnipeg Free Press*, *Kansas City Star* and *Boston Globe*, I certainly could have identified them, given the chance.

John-Paul was very cross that I had been on the street at night, as he said *he* would have been the one to have been accused had I been murdered.

This was not the only attack. I was also knocked down by a group of teenagers close to the St Philip's Street Post Office. They took my purse and handbag while I lay on the ground cradling my stomach in case they kicked me. I managed to stop payment on a small cheque I had been carrying, but I lost an antique flask that I was going to sell, so we had less than ever to eat that day. Out of the evil came goodness. Mrs Evelyn Burnell of Thomas Street heard of the attack and made it her business to speak to me. In the months that followed I don't know what I would have done without her. Way past seventy, and with a pacemaker to stimulate her heart, she had the energy of a much younger woman. I was never hungry again; she saw to that. John-Paul could always go to his Mama for a meal; my family were an ocean away.

Grandmama Evelyn fascinated me with her stories of the roaring twenties and of how she was a Jacksonville pie-maker in the jazz era. She was a great dancer then, and even in 1971 could stand on a chair to show off the old steps.

She hated men, having been deserted by her first husband. The Lord, she said, had punished the whore who had lured him away. The woman apparently forgot her key one day, and as she was climbing through a window it fell like a guillotine. She was quite dead when they found her.

Grandmama's second husband, Samuel Burnelt, failed to live up to her expectations, and he was given his walking papers. Arthur, his successor, fared little better. She threw his clothes into the flooded yard and they floated into the river.

Now, as a deterrent to men, she kept a can of lye and an axe by her bedroom door!

The only man she says she's waiting for now is Jesus. In a world gone mad, Grandmama Evelyn took me to her bosom and loved me like her own child.

Father Stringer continued to write letters to cheer us. The time had come when he and Mother Rutherford could no longer afford the luxury of their dear Elm Close. On 1 June 1971 he wrote:

> I find my cook-housekeeping takes all my time and energy! Your brave letter from Spicers House went to our hearts. What you have been through!
>
> We are thinking what we are going to do. We've been to see one of these Historic Mansions they are dividing into separate apartments for Retired Gentry —Greathead Manor, Lingfield, Surrey—but were rather overwhelmed by it all—except the *Bathroom* which was MUCH too small!

Their house hunting progressed and they had just found a suitable bungalow when Mother Rutherford had another fall. Father Stringer described the accident in a letter written on 27 June with the words *Love to John-Paul* scrawled across the top:

Dawn's our Daughter, and a Dear one,

Margaret read your letter yesterday with great relief and pleasure—how much nicer a Picture and all our congratulations on how you have placed yourselves after so much GRUEL.

We are distressed but bearing up, and Margaret is in a dear little 100 years old Cottage Hospital near by. It IS the other hip that is fractured, but she is making brave progress.

We've got to the 'subject to Contract' stage of selling our House and buying a neighbouring Bungalow—a slightly 'poorer' neighbourhood to please our Accountants, but we look like getting another Mortgage, so there may be the odd Thousands to eat off and pay for our Tax Débâcle—(they've never DEMANDED payment but now it appears we *owe* from 1960! THERE'S 'Accounting' for you!).

I enclose a Fan Letter my Wife has received, I think you will spot its genuin-ness. I have told him I have forwarded his letter to you, but have NOT given him your address—I thought you might like to help in your own time—I THINK it's genuine! But it *reads* very nicely.

Now to decide on which of our LOVED EFFECTS we have to sacrifice!

Thank you dearly for all your love and sympathy— we'll let it become PRACTICAL sympathy, never fear, meanwhile your love and Spirit is quite something!

Yours, near to gibbering, but,
Sincerely, Father Stringer and 'Mother' Rutherford.

CHAPTER TWELVE

The Baby Shower, that traditional American party for expectant mothers, was rather unusual although the guests, including doctors' wives, didn't seem to think so. Sitting receiving their congratulations and little gifts I felt only gratitude that, like Hannah in the Temple, God had at last heard my prayers for a child. A miracle child, John-Paul had called it. I was quite certain that it would be a boy although he had always wanted a baby girl.

The party was arranged by Mrs Ritchia Atkinson who had stood beside me through all my trials. It was given in the home of a mutual friend.

This baby was so wanted, in contrast to the baby I had been. The odd child; the family embarrassment.

When my mother-in-law heard that I was pregnant she hastened to reassure me that other women had been born with similar handicaps to mine and had successfully borne children. My sister-in-law, a nurse at one of the local hospitals, was quick to add that she had known a maternity patient with what appeared to be organs of both sexes, and yet she had given birth to a healthy boy. My sister-in-law had asked the new mother why she had never undergone surgery to 'put things right'.

'My husband has never made the kind of money needed to pay for such an operation,' was the reply.

In my case it was the months of psychiatric treatment that were necessary to fit me for the womanly role so long denied me which had been so costly.

However, my gynaecologist was determined that I should not undergo the mental stress of another miscarriage. I had been so unstable the other time that, for a few hours, kindly friends led me to believe the child had been saved. They did it in order to save my reason, intending to tell me the truth when my mind was able to withstand the sorrow. Unfortunately, one of John-Paul's sisters leaked the false news to a radio station for ten dollars, and the information went around the world. Mother Rutherford told the *News of the World* in London that she was delighted to be a grandmother!

It was all so cruel.

This baby's pregnancy began under somewhat mundane conditions . . . not at all as in the movies where the girl duly collapses and is given a large glass of milk!

I was having coffee in Central Drugs on Meeting Street, when I suddenly became violently sick and slipped off the lunch stool. The lady who presided at the soda fountain immediately took charge of the situation, sending Robert, the delivery man, post-haste for John-Paul. He arrived quite breathless a few minutes later.

After that Mrs Jenness insisted that I give up drinking coffee, which she said wasn't good for anyone in my condition. In its place she substituted tea. I also developed a craving for chocolate ice cream which I had always loathed before.

But to return to my party! As the guests sipped pink champagne I opened their gaily-wrapped packages, containing baby blankets, rubber animals, feeding bowls and cards of safety-pins. I was asked what the new arrival's name would be, but didn't dare tell them what John-Paul had said when I asked him to suggest one. 'I don't care if you call it Coca Cola!'

I liked Jeremy . . . Peter . . . Peregrine—for it was sure to be a boy.

Every night before I went to bed I asked St Teresa of Avila for a boy, but it turned out that she thought otherwise.

Even the coat, bonnet and bootees that I knitted were blue.

I inquired of a doctor friend whether it would be difficult to find a paediatrician to attend the baby. His advice was to register with one in advance. The alternative would be to take the child to the County Emergency Room every time she had a little problem. I therefore 'engaged' the services of a very reputable white paediatrician over the telephone, and upon hearing the Simmons name (a very respectable White surname in Charleston) he agreed to take my unborn child as a patient. However, when he found out that I had a Black Mr Simmons for a husband instead of a White one, his receptionist politely telephoned to tell me that she had made a mistake, that his list was just too crowded to fit my baby in. That kind of doctor I would like to see struck off the medical register!

I next tried a White lady paediatrician of liberal Christian leanings, but she had been so persecuted for undercharging poor Black Mothers that she had been forced out of business.

Finally I heard of the Parkwood Paediatric Group, with offices across the Ashley River. It was a long way to go on foot, but I took an instant liking to Dr Robert F. Marion, a young and progressive paediatrician who immediately put my unborn baby on his list. His name was then sent to the hospital where she would be born, so that he would in due time receive all the necessary information. Dr Marion gave me a number of his excellent leaflets which he had written to help new parents. With Mother Rutherford then very sick in England, and other close relatives far away, this was all a great help, for I had nobody close at hand to answer my baby questions.

Among the poor in Charleston, in whose midst I now lived, there remained much 'voodoo' superstition. One still made visits to the 'root' man or woman who, for a small fee, would dispense charms and advice to the troubled, including expectant mothers. I was soundly chastised by one well-meaning woman for 'viewing the dead' in Fielding's Home for Funerals, because now my child would be 'marked'. In lighter vein, when John-Paul stayed out a few nights I was told quite seriously by a well-meaning woman to bury one of his dirty socks under the back steps, which in future would keep him at home. I know that in England it is said that, if you bury a broad bean, your ugly wart will disappear. So out of curiosity I did what this woman said. It worked! He did sleep home, for a while.

I've always believed that every woman should have a child. Often those who need a baby the most, and would make excellent mothers, never have one. Such women often adopt a child, which is equally satisfying.

When we were first engaged, my husband and I intended to have a family. At that time we thought that the babies would have to be adopted but, to a couple who loved children so much, that did not matter. John-Paul was always taking other people's children out in his car while I envied the young families of my sister and the Burgess cousins.

I've never forgotten a sermon given by Dr John H. Johnson in St Martin's Episcopal Church, New York City. He said that it was every woman's right to have a child of her own, and told us how horrified he had once been to see a new-born infant lying discarded in the gutter.

However, adoption in the United States is not easy. For one thing, each state has its own laws on the subject, and in South Carolina one cannot even apply to adopt a child until one has been married for three years. Out-of-state adoptions are practically an impossibility, since applications would be referred back to the respective South Carolina agencies.

Quite rightly, the prospective parents are carefully investigated on medical, religious, financial and moral grounds. We knew that not in a thousand years would a mixed couple, who had broken unwritten laws by marriage, be granted a child. The authorities would also have looked into John-Paul's private life, and a man who was still seeing a married woman would hardly fit any investigating Baptist pastor's father image!

The shadow of this woman had always hung over my marriage but I had tried to bear it with dignity, not only for myself, but for the sake of the countless Black people who had viewed our marriage with hope, for it had in many ways broken the dark ages of prejudice. Besides, I was not the first woman to have a wandering husband. With my sense of history I recalled that Queen Alexandra had said when her amorous husband, King Edward VII, died '. . . but he loved me best of all'. And I could always console myself with my mother-in-law's

words: 'Always remember that you are *Mrs* Simmons.'
It was me that John-Paul had married. I knew few
Charleston husbands, Black or White, who hadn't
wandered at some time. As John-Paul often reminded
me: 'You have the legal papers.'

CHAPTER THIRTEEN

Back in England Father Stringer had finally sold their beloved Elm Close and purchased a bungalow at Chalfont St Peter. On 1 August 1971, he wrote that:

Yesterday was really quite a climactic day—I got off both Contracts for the sale of Elm Close and the purchase of our new Bungalow near here BY RETURN OF POST with all the Deposit-finding-Bank-overdraft-problems skirted! My Solicitors will be PURRING with content!

Mother Rutherford was still in hospital where the British Prime Minister, Edward Heath, had visited her. Both she and Father Stringer were getting very tired of hospitals. He complained:

Although the physical side of Margaret's recovery seemed to be slow but sure, mentally and psychologically we have both had much to stand up to. I have been driven near crazy by 'NOBODY TELLING ME ANYTHING' and my Doctor NEVER getting in touch with me. At last I declared NEAR-WAR on the SISTER! This has come to a HEAD and, this morning, I AM ACTUALLY GRANTED AN APPOINTMENT WITH THE DOCTOR AND MARGARET TOGETHER!

However, next day he was able to report with some satisfaction:

Margaret had a relapse into sleepiness yesterday but I DID have a good talk with the Doctor, and later a *rapprochment* with the Sister.

Again on 19 December he was writing:

Well! You can't say you don't *live* with us and in our thoughts!

Pat and Molly came and saw Margaret yesterday, Margaret coming out of her 'sleepy' period and enjoying her food and smiling a little and hearing better and responding with more words quite instantly. I have comforted myself, I feel quite legitimately, that a lot of her silence is 'wilful' in the Victorian Nanny sense, while she sorts out Life and Death in her mind and heart, and I feel pretty sure she is still 'having a GO' in the Modern sense. Her GUTS, as ever, leave ME standing, humble, and more deeply in love than ever—satisfied, fulfilled, eternal LOVE.

Victoria Lang-Davis had come to live with them, and was to prove a blessing. To be known as Vicky in the family, in this letter she is charmingly called 'our helpful widow'.

Now it's nearly 8 a.m. I must to my Chores. Our helpful Widow is ensconced with her bird-humouring Cat, she is going to take over her companionship to Margaret functions over the Move restfully and help me with Sorting, Disposing and Arranging. She has Theatrical and professional Musical past-connections and affections, and an amount of Voluntary Hospital work experience.

Well, dear Imaginative and affectionately held Daughter and Son,

Farewell for the present—be seeing you soon, we hope.

Our love
Sincerely
Father Stringer

There was a delightful postscript, which concerned a get-well card I had sent to Mother Rutherford in hospital. It showed a little Black youngster deep in thoughts. He was wearing sneakers. *Thank you for your thinking card!* wrote Father Stringer. *I like his boots!*

It was a great worry to me that when Mother Rutherford and Father Stringer needed me I was unable to be with them. They both insisted that the expected baby come first.

A week before it was born the moment I had dreaded for so long overtook me. Ever since that awful night when John-Paul had told me that another woman was the mother of his son, I had wondered what she looked like. It became such an obsession, I imagined that women I had passed on the street might be she. Then, at last, I saw her under the most embarrassing circumstances. Mrs Simmons, John-Paul's mother, was in hospital. I had visited her on the Wednesday at which time she made me promise to return the next evening. On my way there a sudden freak storm broke, flooding the streets so that I had to hold my shoes and in stockinged feet wade to higher ground. Soaking wet I arrived at the hospital, only to be told that 'I' was already there—that Mr John-Paul Simmons and his 'wife' were with his mother.

I suppose I should have turned around; gone home

and never have seen him again. Instead I went up to Mrs Simmons' room with a hospital guard, who insisted upon accompanying me. And there I saw them.

My husband was wearing a tweed sports jacket. I've never liked tweed since. Upon seeing her I thought of that famous scene in Somerset Maugham's *The Letter*, where Lesley confronts her lover's Eurasian wife. Perhaps I had expected too much, a great beauty, a rival in the real sense of the word. Instead, one look was enough for me to know that I could hold my own beside her.

John-Paul was furious because his two lives had suddenly come together. I thought that John-Paul would never come home again; that he would not want to face me. I was wrong. Three days later he was back and in my bed, seemingly oblivious to what had happened. Maybe I just bring out the worst in men!

The reaction to the hospital encounter was sickness. I felt as I always do when there is a death in the family: a nauseating emptiness inside.

On the following Sunday I went to lunch with West Grant, but I felt so ill that I could eat nothing. I was burning hot, glassy-eyed and in great discomfort. I lay on West's sofa while he phoned the doctor. As evening came on I felt better and returned home.

There was to be little peace. Somebody gave me a bad cheque and more money was needed for the hospital. Desperate, I called in Dr Luther Martin, who bought my family console table and Italian commode. I hated to see them go, but I thought of what my cousin Isabel Lydia Whitney had once told me: 'Possessions are only material.'

For safety's sake the baby was to be born at the University of Pennsylvania Hospital in Philadelphia. I had been warned by two close friends how much publicity would result had the birth been in Charleston. For further privacy I was registered under an assumed name.

John-Paul was very tied up with his boat, but he did come to see me off. He was very kind and held me in his arms for a few minutes. Larry Shelton, another friend, drove me to the airport and put me safely on the plane.

As there was no telephone at Spicers House it was arranged that I should contact 'Mr James'—James Fickling—the genial butler at our Society Street home, who had a telephone and knew how to get in touch with John-Paul.

I was a wreck when I was finally admitted to the hospital in Philadelphia. My whole body seemed to wrack with pain; my mind was fuzzy.

It was a little girl. Well, John-Paul would be pleased, I thought. He loved little girls. She might be brilliant like V. Sackville-West, who had helped me so much with my writing. Then I thought of Bette Davis and what she had said to her husband when she gave birth to her first child at thirty-nine: 'You married an old woman and she has given you a daughter.'

And a blessing that daughter would be. As Lady Rosamund Fisher, widow of Lord Fisher of Lambeth, former Archbishop of Canterbury, wrote to me: 'She will be your joy.'

She was a beautiful baby; she has always been embarrassingly beautiful. And she had John-Paul's bow legs!

* * *

... For one long, confused moment I hardly knew whether I was looking at the broken body of my dog or at my baby. I sat up, realizing I was on the cold kitchen floor of Spicers House, and that my faithful guard dog, Jackie, was lying there imploringly, her hind-leg bowed and obviously broken. I knew that she needed help, and I knew that I did also.

I dismissed the past. From that moment on my thoughts were pitched ahead, towards escape. If it had only been a question of my own safety and sanity I would have shrugged and gone on, my head held high as before.

But now I had Natasha to think of. My responsibility was to her.

Book Two

CHAPTER ONE

I was determined not to act in haste. Somehow I had to create an opportunity for us all, including John-Paul, to leave Charleston. But I knew it would be difficult to persuade John-Paul to go. He would have thought it was running away.

The next thing that happened was John-Paul's arrival, in an awful state, begging me, for our safety, to leave with the child.

'I don't want anything to happen to either of you,' he said. He then made an amazing statement: a relative had told him that a Welfare Department worker had called me 'an unfit mother'.

That was all I needed. I thought of my Mother Rutherford, and marched, as she would have done, to the Welfare Department, carrying Natasha in a shawl. On arrival everyone in the office asked for my autograph! They were wonderful, Black and White, a splendid example of people working together as a unit. The social worker I saw was Black. She told me that the person who had made the remark was a liar; that nobody could take Natasha away from me, for in South Carolina preference is always given to the mother. They all thought that Natasha was a lovely child, and ever since kept a loving eye upon us. Mrs Janice McInness, my special social worker, became more than a friend. She was never too busy to listen.

On leaving the Welfare Department that day I went straight to the F.B.I., where, as always, I was properly treated. I reported that I was threatened, and by whom. They assured me that nobody could 'put me away' and take Natasha; that if the threats continued I had only to lift a telephone and call them. I then went back to Spicers House, sold a French marble mantelpiece, worth $2,500, for only $200, and with Natasha flew to New York, where for two weeks I lived in seclusion at the Prince George Hotel. I just needed peace and time to think.

On returning to Charleston all was quiet. I stayed with friends for a few days while we made Spicers House a little more habitable. Jackie was still very ill, and I brought her home from the animal hospital to nurse her, because I loved her.

On Sunday afternoons I went to work in Larry Shelton's antique shop on Folly Road. Usually Natasha went with me, sleeping in a cupboard drawer, for we badly needed the money, but on one occasion I left her with friends as it was so cold. When I got back, there was John-Paul, and he had Natasha all dressed up like a little doll sitting in the carry-cot that the waitresses, owners and friends at Yip's Restaurant had made a collection to buy for her. The same had happened at Frieda's Restaurant on Society Street. Their staff gave her nightclothes.

We spent such a happy evening, and I hated to see John-Paul go. He was still working on the sewer tunnel. Next evening he turned up again, all covered with wet sand from the bowels of the earth. He asked us to go home with him and we did. He held my hand and was asking people on the street, 'You know my old lady, don't you?'

At this time two fine Charleston ladies, Florence Haskell and Miriam Long, were bringing food parcels and gifts of clothing for the baby and me. Suddenly they began to receive phone calls threatening bodily harm if they continued to do so. I couldn't understand the mind of anybody who would want to harm these innocent women, especially at Christmas-time.

Because of all the dangers I decided that Natasha must be baptized immediately. I am of the Anglican faith and have very definite religious beliefs. I went to the office of the Episcopal Cathedral Church of St Luke and St Paul to make the arrangements. I had Natasha cooing in my arms, and the lady in the office said she would get in touch with me. But she didn't. As it happens, Natasha was finally baptized at St Clement's Church, Hastings, where the Blessing of my marriage to John-Paul took place. So much for an 'unwanted' Christian baby!

Jackie lingered on until 23 December. Early that morning I was woken by the howl of a dog. 'Peter,' I said, for I could always identify our dogs by their bark. But Peter, Jackie's husband, had died months before! Then I heard Jackie give an answering howl. I rushed downstairs to find the gentle creature, who had suffered so much for me, dead at the foot of the stairs. I like to think that Peter came for her.

It was a sad Christmas. Little Annette Waites came in to help me decorate a tree for Natasha, who seemed to know it was for her. I took a picture of my child asleep on Christmas Eve. She seemed happy and content, a reminder of the Holy Babe on that first Christmas at

Bethlehem. Then, on Christmas morning, John-Paul's mother sent a message for the baby and me, asking us to dinner.

I had sold a necklace to buy Natasha a fine baby carriage, one that later on could be converted into a stroller. John-Paul came to fetch us, and it was the happiest moment of my life to see him, dressed in a sailor's short navy-blue jacket, taking his daughter to visit his mother. Some men might feel silly pushing a baby carriage, but not John-Paul!

Our marriage, with all its ups and downs, has had many precious moments, but none more beautiful than this.

CHAPTER TWO

Mother Rutherford was back in hospital. She found hospital life excessively trying, and so did Father Stringer. He lived for the moment when he might bring her home to Hatfield, the new bungalow they had bought at Chalfont St Peter. He had been especially incensed by the telephone threats to my friends who had been sending me food and clothing. I tried to reassure him that we had many friends in Charleston, that it was only our enemies who were racists and hypocrites.

In an undated letter written on MARGARET RUTHERFORD letterhead he touched on the subject of racialism, Black Power and Old Age.

I don't know HOW to thank you for your letter of the 4th, safely arrived! There is so much sadness in it, although it starts off with so lovely a description of Natasha!

We do want to hear how John-Paul is faring, he must be feeling quite stricken for you, and for his own people.

I have, unhappily, met White Colonies of individuals over the World who I could readily describe as 'making Whites STINK in Native nostrils'. Cyprus was one of them, and the Seychelle Islands were also so described to me by a Militant Suffragist Maiden Resident Aunt! In South Africa I gather there are others. And now your Charleston! I don't see that they serve the World's purpose in any shape or way. I'd rather have Black Power—at least THEY clarify the issues and one respects that even in an Enemy!

I hope by now you will have received my letter giving you the news of my Move and preparations for Margaret's welcome Home shortly we pray. However be-Nursed and carried about, Doctor agrees that a return to HOME LIFE will be our mental and spiritual betterment. We have got sick of never speaking to each other IN PRIVATE!

Patrick and Ethel were coming to lunch yesterday and I was going to give him your sad news, but at the last moment he didn't think his Mother was fit enough; it was a bitter disappointment—I do want this Bungalow to be ALIVE with our friends for Margaret to come back to from her long Public Sojourn, but ALL our friends now seem to be Old and hampered too! I suppose it's all part of this Loneliness of Old Age we're hearing about!

At last he was allowed to bring her home to the new bungalow with the room he had prepared with such loving care. There was a continuous parade of nurses, none of whom stopped very long. A formidable pair of lesbian nurses lifted the invalid in to their little car and took her for a ride through the familiar Buckinghamshire countryside, which she seemed to enjoy very much. The nursing profession and Father Stringer seemed always at odds. One of their number called him a 'silly old man'. 'Perhaps I was a silly old man,' he later told me, 'but nobody was going to keep me out of my wife's room.' On 12 April 1972, he wrote:

I am a little distracted with grief at Margaret's continued helplessness, and fussed by Nurses.

Margaret is not reading or writing and only talking a little and we have few visitors, but the bungalow is a comfort and I can't believe we won't be having more fun soon.

It was a lovely spring, and they were able to eat out in the garden. He pushed her about in a wheelchair and the children from the new housing estate opposite were very friendly and kind. They demonstrated their new space guns to Mother Rutherford.

They were looking forward to our proposed visit to England, and Father Stringer wrote: 'How glad we are you'll soon be over here, with John-Paul, Natasha and all sorts of Rutherford-Davises!' Rutherford-Davis being, of course, their namesake and our much beloved chihuahua terrier.

Mother Rutherford was especially delighted when Charlie Chaplin returned to America and was given an Oscar. For not only did both veteran comedians much admire each other's talents, but Mother Rutherford had played in Chaplin's movie, *The Countess from Hong Kong*.

By this time I had persuaded John-Paul to come to England with us—at least for a time—for I was very near a breakdown. Not only were we still distraught at losing our beloved house on Society Street, but the building inspector who had made our lives a misery there was now harrying us to make instant repairs to Spicers House, on which we had not even closed. Of course it needed repairing but we had no money left to do it. We had had to pay twenty-five hundred dollars merely on an option to buy and it was costing us a further hundred dollars a month just for the privilege of staying there.

Knowing our plight, my family in England were now pressing John-Paul to give up the struggle in Charleston and to join them. They wanted to set John-Paul up with his own garage, or, if he preferred the sea, to help us settle in Hastings where there were many boats and fellow fishermen.

At last, a decision was made to leave. We applied to the British Consul in Atlanta, who was very helpful, and who arranged for our remaining faithful dogs— Rutherford-Davis, Lizzie Wormulus and Emily Louisa the chihuahuas, and the Ubangi, Banji—to travel also, and to go into the necessary six months' quarantine. The poor dogs! Having shared so much of our misery, like me they were very thin. The Consul also informed me that John-Paul would be granted a work permit.

All seemed to be going well when literally at the last moment my husband decided not to go. I think that leaving the other child was the real reason—he has always had a conscience. The last few days before our departure without him were a nightmare. Neither of us had enough to eat and the will to work seemed to have left both John-Paul and myself. We were temporarily defeated.

I existed through the slowly passing days, almost unable to feel, incapable of making plans and beginning to despair that our lives would ever change—either for good or ill. Then came the awful night when John-Paul came in very excited and seemingly possessed by the same evil spirit that had surfaced the night of our engagement when, without any warning, he had attacked me. This time I was in bed, with Natasha beside me in her cradle.

'I'm going to get my son,' he cried. I was half asleep, but knowing that he was temporarily on bad terms with the child's mother, and fearing a disturbance in which somebody would be hurt, I tried to persuade him not to go out in the middle of the night. But as it turned out the only person to be hurt was me!

Enraged by my efforts to pacify him, he leapt on to the bed and grabbed my throat, straddling me with his body that then weighed nearly two hundred pounds.

'You don't want me to have my son,' he screamed, but I had no chance to answer. 'This is the end,' I thought, as he pressed his strong fingers into my throat. There was a deathly silence; the silence of the tomb. Everything was a grey-green sea. 'I am dead,' I thought, and then I realized I was still in my bedroom and that John-Paul was crying.

If I can hear him weep and recognize where I am then my soul has not left my body, I reasoned.

Then, as I watched, powerlessly, and as though paralysed, from a great distance, he took Natasha from the cradle and laid her beside me. 'Now we'll all be dead together,' he mumbled.

'John-Paul, I'm not dead,' I struggled to reassure him, but the words came painfully. There was blood all over my throat and across my breasts, and my nightgown was soaked with it. In a frenzy of contrition he tried to pull a dress over my shoulders, finally succeeding, although he'd put it on back to front. Then, vowing that he was going to take me to the Emergency Room at Charleston County Hospital, he half pulled, half carried me into the street.

I pleaded with him to do no such thing. I tried to make him understand that there would be a police report and that he would be arrested. But steadfastly he refused to listen. Thank God we did not meet a police patrol, for by the time we had reached Smith Street the cold air had sobered him. At last I was able to persuade my husband to take me home. Grandmama Evelyn and Rosabelle Ten Cents Waites, her daughter, cleaned my wounds and washed my nightgown. I could not be seen for three days. But during all that time, John-Paul nursed me with great tenderness, changed Natasha's diapers and saw to her feeding.

CHAPTER THREE

While I continued to arrange the move to England the news from Gerrards Cross became less good. Mother Rutherford's condition gradually deteriorated. The fall she had sustained while filming *Arabella* in Italy was to be the beginning of the end.

Her worsening condition is best described by Father Stringer, who wrote on 12 April 1972.

> I am a little distracted with grief at Margaret's continued helplessness and fussed by Nurses and I can't remember when I last wrote to you.

Yet even in her eventide there were some consolations. Father Stringer was simply wonderful. Theirs was a great love and the knowledge of that love sustained me throughout my own tribulations.

Even in his obvious distress he was able in the same letter cheerily to recall the fun he and Mother Rutherford had had when the opening sequence of *Murder, She Said*, the first of the Agatha Christie Miss Marple detective movies, had had to be retaken on No 1 Platform at Paddington. Delighted schoolchildren, and some grown-ups, had interrupted filming to ask for autographs.

They were both very pleased that in Germany she was to find a whole new audience when her many movies were shown for the first time on that country's television. Her new fans voted her to be the most popular actress of the year.

They found much comfort in their new home, Hatfield, which had a sweet garden with forty very talkative doves. Inside the house Father Stringer and Vicky Lang-Davis lovingly arranged all the little treasures and awards that Mother Rutherford had collected during her long acting career.

There was to be just one other letter from them which concluded with the words: 'We are longing to see you both walk down our garden path with Natasha.'

They so longed to see their granddaughter.

Then came the end!

West Grant telephoned with the news of Mother Rutherford's passing. He was very kind, first asking if I had been listening to the morning news on the radio. I said that I hadn't, so he told me to sit down. Then he quietly told me that our darling had left us. After that, the telephone kept ringing with messages of condolence from all over the United States and Canada. I tried to keep up my end in America just as I would have done in England. I put on a black dress, and holding my baby received them—a surprising number of callers.

The Charleston *News and Courier*, who had published an account of my marriage on the Obituary page, signifying, I suppose, that I was dead to society, published an editorial extolling Margaret Rutherford, the actress. They deliberately failed, however, to mention what was surely of local interest . . . that the adopted daughter she loved lived in Charleston.

Mother Rutherford would never have approved of that! I wondered who had written the editorial, recalling how at Charleston's Arcade Theater I had sat beside Peter Manigault, president of that same newspaper, to watch one of Mother Rutherford's movies.

The *New York Times* redressed the injustice by running a factual and full obituary in which they noted that Dame Margaret Rutherford and Stringer Davis had four adopted children ... and that I had married John-Paul with her full consent.

During the days that followed my heart was with Father Stringer in his grief, though I was prevented from being with him in person. My passport still had to go the U.S. Passport Office at Miami to have Natasha's photograph and vital statistics attached. I could not have travelled with her to the funeral unless this was done. Even had I left her behind—and I would not—there was nobody who could guarantee her safety. The memory of the threats to put me away in order to steal her and my royalties was still seared on my mind. I grieved, although I knew Father Stringer would understand. Above all, Natasha had to be protected. Besides, I tried to reason with myself, when all the publicity and excitement surrounding the funeral was over, surely that was the time when I might be most comfort to him. And happily, as it turned out, I was right.

Mother Rutherford's funeral service was held in St James's Church, Gerrards Cross, on 25 May 1972. Robert Morley, who had co-starred with her in *Murder at the Gallop* and in other successes, gave the address. Robert Eddison read Henry Vaughan's 'They are all gone into the world of light'.

Father Stringer chose the hymns: 'The Lord's My Shepherd, I'll not want', 'Now Thank We All Our God', and, by coincidence, one of our wedding hymns: 'Love Divine, All Loves Excelling'.

As they carried her into the churchyard the *Nunc Dimittis* . . . 'Lord, now lettest thou thy servant depart in peace . . .' was chanted.

Afterwards Father Stringer wrote us: 'I couldn't believe it was going to happen and I can't yet realize it has.'

CHAPTER FOUR

John-Paul and I both seemed to have fallen into a kind of despair. Lost without his beloved boat, which he had sold in a fit of despond, he sat in a chair just staring into space. His idea of feeding us was to go and catch some fish. Unfortunately I never much cared for fish.

But since babies need milk I pushed Natasha to King Street in the baby carriage every day to make a little money. We sold bric-à-brac, books; whatever was small enough to carry.

As Father Stringer continued to write sad letters, my thoughts turned increasingly to England and to home.

With John-Paul in such a state of melancholia my nerves were close to snapping. We talked it over and both decided that it might be the wisest thing for me to leave Charleston with the baby, if only for a rest.

In due course our dogs were examined by a veterinary surgeon, pronounced to be in good health, taken to Charleston Airport, fitted with travelling kennels, and were flown off to England. Next morning a call came from National Airlines to say Banji had died *en route*. It was a blow; dear, faithful Banji. First it had been Jackie; now both my guard dogs were gone. I feared for our other dogs also who were being held in New York City until an autopsy could be performed on Banji to see that whatever had caused his death was not contagious.

When the cause of Banji's death was discovered to be

hepatitis, the chihuahuas were reprieved and allowed to continue their journey to England.

John-Paul still sat silently in his chair, did not wash nor care about anything. I felt on the verge of collapse. Natasha's large birth certificate had now arrived from Harrisburg, Pennsylvania, where it had been delayed, and my passport was duly amended to include her.

I had to get away. Even John-Paul saw that . . . or at least I thought he did.

It was now decided that he should continue to live in Spicers House while Natasha and I were away. I would hope to regain my health, then examine the possibilities of setting up home for ourselves in England. I felt it would be safe to leave him for, as I have already said, we had paid a generous option to buy Spicers House. I would leave him a room full of furniture, a bed, my valuable Charleston-made writing desk, a new sofa, chairs, etc. All his fishing permits and private papers would be together on the desk. Everything seemed to be going smoothly. He would not be lonely for we had been parted before. There was no ill feeling. I had sold some furniture to pay the fares. He could follow at any time, or I could return.

Then the demon that possessed him struck once more. Late one night he ran into the house, took the sleeping child out of her cot and ran off with her.

He was in such a distraught state that I feared for his life as well as the child's. The local police helped search. We went first to his mother's home and were informed they were not there. (Months later he was to tell me that they were hiding in a back room.) We called at the home of his little son and I was told that they might be hiding on the docks. They were not.

I have never known such a long and awful night. I sat on the porch with Grandmama Evelyn waiting for news. As dawn came the air was filled with heart-rending screams, coming from Spicers House just down the street. I knew that they were the screams of my child.

Grandmama Evelyn called the police, who said that I must not enter my home alone. Three squadrons of officers arrived and, guns drawn, they entered the almost empty house.

Upstairs they found Natasha screaming in her cot. There was no sign of her father.

For three days I lay in a stupor at Grandmama Evelyn's. I cried and cried while she kept telling me that I had to live for my child. I longed to see my husband. I wanted to look for him. To go away under such circumstances and maybe never see him again was terrible to contemplate.

The police said that in our own interest we must not try to find him. Grandmama Evelyn helped pack our clothes, then on the fourth day, Daddy-O Coakley, one of the neighbours, drove us to the airport.

I sent John-Paul a letter, care of Captain Glover Hayes, an old netmaker who loved us both. I had to tell him that we still wanted and needed him; that nobody more than he knew how much I needed to rest.

Having heard a rumour that I had left John-Paul, a local pressman sent a message that newsmen would meet me in New York. Thank God there was some kind of newspaper strike! Natasha and I boarded the jumbo jet for home without publicity.

Natasha and I were both exhausted. She slept all the way in the cot provided by the airlines and had to be awakened and dressed before landing. We took a taxi to the Hotel Washington in London which was to be our headquarters for the next five weeks.

I telephoned Father Stringer to let him know we had arrived, and also my sister at Sissinghurst and Aunty Babs (Mrs Ernest Burgess) at Eastbourne. Then I went to bed. I was still tired out. I needed time to think.

I felt better next morning, while Natasha seemed none the worse for her long journey plus the six hours difference in time. Leaving sub-tropical Charleston for a chilly English summer, we both had put on woollies.

After a marvellous breakfast at which I introduced Natasha to an English kipper, we set out for Marylebone station and Gerrards Cross. Natasha, still unable to walk, had to be carried, although I had brought a small springless stroller with us from America. She looked a picture in her large old-fashioned white Charleston sunbonnet, and people made pleasing comments as we passed.

My thoughts were constantly on my husband whom I had never wished to leave. As we passed by Marylebone parish church *en route* for the station, I thought with added poignancy of Robert Browning and Elizabeth Barrett, those fabled lovers who had married there.

My mind went back to Mother Rutherford's reading Elizabeth's famous poem at our Hastings wedding:

How do I love thee? Let me count the ways . . .

and to the Reverend Thomas Savins' reading from the *Song of Songs* at our second wedding:

Many waters cannot quench love.
Neither can the floods drown it;

If a man would give all the substance of his house
   for love,
It would utterly be contemned.

So much had happened since that beautiful day. I
decided not to tell Father Stringer of our strange part-
ing, for he loved my husband so much.

These thoughts comforted me, and I needed comfort.
For when we purchased our train ticket from a Black
window clerk, Natasha called him 'Dadda'.

Natasha enjoyed her first ride on an English train,
while the green fields of Buckinghamshire gave me
much needed solace and a sense of peace. But the
moment I dreaded came too soon. As the train drew
into Gerrards Cross station I feared how different it
would be this time...there would be no Mother
Rutherford with puckered nose and dancing chin to
greet me. Oh how I wished that she could have lived
a little longer and seen Natasha: but at least she had
enjoyed her first photographs.

The train jolted to a halt. I managed to get off in one
piece clutching Natasha, a large bag filled with baby
paraphernalia, and a bunch of mixed asters for Mother
Rutherford's grave. How I had managed to protect
their large purple petals and yellow centres from
Natasha's little fingers was a miracle.

Then I saw him, much older, his shoulders stooped
...dear, faithful Father Stringer who had loved
Mother Rutherford so much. And she him. 'Without
him I am nothing,' she had written at the beginning of
her autobiography.

He kissed us both profusely. 'Oh, I do wish that
John-Paul could have come as well,' he said.

The first thing we did was to drive to Mother Rutherford's grave in Gerrards Cross churchyard, a peaceful spot surrounded by an arboretum.

She was buried under an enormous blue spruce, the species that grow naturally in Colorado. The graves were arranged like the rays of the sun around its trunk.

How appropriate, I thought, for in life she had loved trees so much, even in wintertime when they were bare.

'She enriched the English language,' Father Stringer said, 'and now she rests in English soil. Friendly American pilgrims will also find her grave.'

Blue lobelia and old-fashioned salmon-red begonias brightened the blessed spot. We said a little prayer, then I took a photograph of Father Stringer and Natasha holdings hands before we left for Hatfield in Mrs Jones's taxi. Mrs Jones had driven us all in happier days, the last time being to my autographing party.

We both looked instinctively at our old home, dear Elm Close, as we passed the holly hedge. 'A nice man bought it, if that's any consolation,' said Father Stringer . . . 'and he has put up rather a nice front gate.'

The new bungalow was perched at the top of Joiner's Lane . . . a very hilly spot. From the garden one could glimpse the rolling countryside where Mother Rutherford had been able to relax after long hours spent at the film studio. A flock of doves swooped down from the roof to salute our arrival, two of them being particularly vocal.

Father Stringer apologized. 'Why Noah chose a dove as the symbol of peace, I'll never know, for they are the noisiest things.'

On entering I saw Minnie and Nicodemus, and a

wave of emotion came over me. Minnie was the little stuffed white rabbit with the blue satin cape who travelled everywhere with Mother Rutherford; Nicodemus a stuffed black cat. If either of my adoptive parents felt a little tired and out of sorts, instead of getting grumpy with each other, he or she would say to the other, 'Minnie doesn't feel like talking this morning.' It was such a kind, civilized way of expressing one's cross feelings! Minnie and Nicodemus looked so lonely and forlorn that I was glad I had brought along their Cousin Augusta the Elephant and Olaf the Unicorn to cheer them up. Cousin Augusta was rescued from the glass showcase of a gift stand in Boston Railroad Station, while Olaf arrived with a piece of yellow wool sticking out of his forehead. Mother Rutherford had given one glance at him and pronounced: 'Why, look at his head! Of course, he's a unicorn.'

There were photographs everywhere in the 'sanctuary', which was what Father Stringer called the sitting-room. He placed the large photograph of myself holding Natasha, aged two weeks, on the piano beside those of Mother Rutherford and their dear friend Ivor Novello, the actor and composer. Opposite, the Oscar statuette gazed at us all very benevolently.

Tea was delightful. Vicky Lang-Davis had prepared it so daintily, and Father Stringer had gone into the village to pick out the cakes!

Outside, the doves had suddenly become quiet as if they were aware it was teatime and the humans' turn to talk. Natasha nibbled on a buttered scone, then joined Peter, the black puppy, on the sofa. Father Stringer tucked Mother Rutherford's big shawl around them.

We had truly come home.

Then he played one of his own little compositions on the upright piano. 'Now this one is for John-Paul,' he said. Then later, writing my husband a little note, he said:

I was so sorry not to see you, and do hope we may see you again soon. Dawn gave me a lovely picture of Natasha, which I have put on my piano, to remind me of how much you enjoyed my playing!

Suddenly it had turned very cold; it was evening. I missed John-Paul so much. We couldn't get a taxi and had to walk down the hill which was all torn up by bulldozers. I was afraid that Natasha would catch cold after leaving so hot a climate, so that in desperation I hailed a police car and explained the situation. 'Jump in, Madam,' said the cheerful policeman. Father Stringer came too.

As we arrived at the station the train for London drew into the platform. We called out and it waited! After kissing us both, Father Stringer doffed his hat and gave a very theatrical bow to the engine driver for being such a considerate gentleman.

Our next safari was to Sissinghurst to see my natural father Jack, my sister Fay, and of course to visit Margie's grave. It is always such a pleasure to go by train into Kent, the Garden of England. Natasha slept most of the way. We managed to share a taxi from Staplehurst Station to Sissinghurst, a few miles distant. Jack was very pleased to see us. It seemed to me that he had failed much since my last visit, with Nancy O. Basey. He was still on crutches. Billie, his dog, formerly

Sir Harold Nicolson's, was having heart-attacks. All was decay.

Jack and Natasha seemed to take an instant liking to each other. He had been good with all children—except with me. When I asked if he would mind her for a little while so that I might go and buy some flowers for Margie's grave, his face lit up with pleasure.

'You mean you would let me?' he asked.

'Of course,' I said. 'You are her grandfather.'

Natasha was having a fine time when I left. Billie was a great incentive, as she has always loved animals. I felt that she missed Rutherford-Davis, then in quarantine, very much.

I walked up Mill Lane to buy my flowers. There was smell of bonfire ash in the air, while the English country road hurt my feet. It all seemed part of a lovely dream . . . roses in the cottage gardens . . . and above all a continuing sense of peace. I was beginning to relax; that fear which had become part of my life in Charleston was disappearing.

When I returned to the cottage Jack was teaching Natasha how to blow kisses.

Fay arrived, clutched my child to her bosom and asked if she'd had enough to eat. She insisted that I buy some special baby food (which Natasha hated). It was so funny, Natasha has always been a very healthy child! Grandmama Evelyn had been feeding her for some time from the table.

I left them to carry the baby through the village to the cemetery and propped her up against darling Margie's cross to have her picture taken. It was a great moment. Natasha plucked at the flowers.

Next day we went to Bromley to see my Burgess

cousins. The Derek Ivings children (Patricia Burgess is their mother). Yvette and the twins Karl and Gregg immediately took charge of Natasha. They borrowed a baby carriage and introduced her to the neighbourhood. Their parents drove us to see Maureen, Nigel Burgess's wife. Pat and Maureen were to be two of Natasha's godmothers, Maureen having promised to look after Natasha should anything happen to John-Paul or me.

Cousin Peter, his wife Jean, and their family were on holiday so we did not see them, while Cousin Sally was expecting another baby any day. Her two little boys, Todd and Kirk, gave Natasha a model racing car. She wasn't yet able to walk, but she could crawl, and joined in floor games with all her English cousins until she fell asleep from sheer exhaustion. The Ivings drove us back to the Washington Hotel, then we had a late supper together in Shepherd Market.

A writing assignment had been obtained for me, and this entailed my staying in London. My long-time friend Patsy Turner Behr and her son Digby often came to see us. They arranged little Saturday trips into the park so that Natasha might feed the ducks. On one memorable safari with them by train to Chingford, Essex, we went to see Rutherford-Davis 'in jail'. Rutherford was led into the exercise yard, while Emily Louisa tried to escape from her kennel to follow. Both dogs were in excellent condition; they had gained weight and were beautifully groomed. I believe that the quarantine confinement saved their lives.

Natasha cried so much when she had to leave her 'Ruthy' behind that one of my London editor friends insisted upon buying her another dog. A pet-shop in Shepherd Market was displaying a window full of puppies. I was terrified that she might choose a Great Dane, since we were living in a hotel! Thank goodness the tiniest dog, a tan-coloured chihuahua who was chasing a tiny red ball, caught her eye. That was how we first met Isadora. Isadora and her new mistress became instant friends; Natasha went to sleep that night clutching the new puppy who seemed very much at home. She called her 'Issy'.

Every morning Natasha and I would take a walk in Green Park where her old-fashioned red sun-bonnet was much admired. She had a little round face then, and a big smile for everybody. One afternoon I pushed her towards Buckingham Palace but there was little peace in that direction. Only in Detroit have I seen so many cars at one time, while the stench of gasoline was most unpleasant. I felt quite sorry for the Queen.

We paid two delightful visits to Kew Gardens, folding up the stroller and taking the underground. For only fifteen new pence we seemed back in the Victorian era as we walked down an unspoiled country lane to Queen's Cottage. (Queen Victoria had donated the cottage surroundings with the wise stipulation that they should be left in their original wild state.)

Natasha was photographed in front of the Great Pagoda feeding more exotic Chinese ducks.

With stroller squeaking we entered the Great Palm House known as 'the stove', and were nearly cooked! Natasha was perspiring like a San Francisco fog. As we hastened to get outside before she contracted pneumonia, a young woman ran up and kissed her. It was my cousin Julia and her Australian husband Barry

Long, whom I had never met. The world is surely a very small place!

There was no news from Charleston. We religiously mailed John-Paul cards and letters, but had no response. Once, Rosabelle, Grandmama Evelyn's daughter, telephoned in the middle of the night; my heart leapt when the overseas operator spoke. I thought that it might have been my husband. But her news was not good. Spicers House had been boarded up; John-Paul had been seen sitting on the doorstep.

I immediately xeroxed copies of the receipts for moneys we had paid on the house to John-Paul and to his parents, advising them to see Brantley Seymour, my lawyer, at once.

Weeks passed before I found out that John-Paul had come home to find the house padlocked. He could not even get his clothes. About a thousand dollars' worth of furniture 'disappeared' and has never been seen since.

I did investigate the possibility of apartments in London, but they were very expensive. I had never asked my relatives for a penny in my life and did not intend to do so now. But with a nine-month-old daughter to support I had to make a living somehow. I was a teenager when I first went to America. Ironically, I knew the New York literary world better than London's. Then, after raising so many hopes of work, my new literary agent abandoned me. I realized that I had been away from home too long.

One night, after seeing the Black movie *Nothing But a Man* on television, I was so overcome with longing to see my husband that I booked our air passage back to

America. I had one month before our departure, and I decided to live in Eastbourne, where I had been happy as a child. We had a small furnished apartment on the fifth floor overlooking the pier. There was no elevator, which was rather hard on Margie's sister, Aunty Babs, when she came to see us.

I enjoyed the stay in Eastbourne with its many thrift and antique shops. An English lady, Mrs Daisy Karet, who was living in the Braemar Hotel close by, was very kind and motherly to us. She was a great help supervising the tea for Natasha's christening, which was to be the great event of this period.

On the day Father Stringer travelled down by the train on his own. His fits of crying and melancholia over Mother Rutherford's death seemed to have abated. After Natasha had introduced him to Isadora we had a lovely lunch together in the Braemar dining-room. Little did I think it would be the last day in this life that we would be together.

He had brought Natasha a silver christening bowl and with a sweet letter which read:

For the Late Margaret Rutherford, OBE
Gerrards Cross

Sept. 17th 1972

Dear Dawn

This is surely one day when dear 'Mother' and 'Father' can be with Natasha, you and please God John-Paul in the Love of the Lord.

Blessings ever,

Stringer

Cousin Rosamanda made the christening cake but because of a thrombosis in her leg she was absent from the ceremony. This was disappointment, for she had been the favourite lady fireman cousin of my childhood, and, of course, matron of honour at my Hastings wedding.

Natasha wore a lace dress trimmed with tiny seed pearls made by Margie's cousin, Mrs David Chisolm of Montreal, Canada, and a lace poke bonnet. I had a yellow linen dress, and as I could not find a suitable hat I wore a piece of fine white lace on my head.

Sheila Littleton, an antiques connoisseur of Tunbridge Wells, Franklyn Lenthall, a Broadway producer, Anthony Dawson, the movie star, Philip Savins, the rector's son, and my cousins Patricia and Derek Ivings and Maureen Burgess were godparents. Natasha, who was baptized by the Reverend Thomas Savins (who had married John-Paul and me) managed to kick a white kid shoe into the font. During the ceremony I was given a candle to hold, and afterwards, when the register was signed, I gave 'Fisherman' as John-Paul's occupation.

'Very appropriate,' said the Reverend Mr Savins, for St Clement's overlooks the sea.

Patricia and Maureen brought lots of good things for the christening tea, while Aunty Babs and Uncle Ernie supplied enormous white chrysanthemums for the table.

Father Stringer thoroughly enjoyed facing the cameras again, standing next to me in the christening pictures. We put our arms round each other as I walked him to the door where a taxi was waiting. The final curtain was soon to fall. I never saw him again.

CHAPTER FIVE

Natasha and I flew back to America, taking Isadora the chihuahua in a small cardboard kennel. It was a pleasant, lazy flight with lots of good things to eat. Natasha adored the Black steward who carried her around to meet everybody aboard.

We arrived in Charleston late at night and very tired. Larry Shelton met us and drove us to a local hotel. Since it was not far from Captain Glover Hayes' little house, and I thought he would know where we could find John-Paul, I went over there immediately. The house was in darkness; later I heard that the Captain was in hospital.

Turning on to Thomas Street, Gussie Mae, the corgi, knew my footsteps, and ran yapping to greet me. She was still guarding the sad, boarded-up house.

Grandmama Evelyn could hardly believe her own eyes when she saw us.

Next day we called upon John-Paul's mother to learn his whereabouts. Mrs Simmons' immediate reaction was, 'I didn't expect to see you again. Who will pay for my carpet now?'

Apparently that was what my husband was buying her.

She did, however, get a message to John-Paul who, after the indignity of being locked out, had found a job on the docks with Richard's Launch Service. He turned up at the motel that night with an enormous dog that looked like Lassie. It was a very happy reunion.

He told me that all our belongings at Spicers House had disappeared. Later, a friend, Jaime Westendorff, told me that a realtor was showing him and two friends over Spicers House when he noticed our brand new sofa. 'Why ever would they leave a new sofa behind?' he had asked. Three days later he returned with the same realtor but the sofa was missing. 'What happened to the sofa?' he had inquired. 'What sofa?' came the reply. Jaime did not buy the property.

I was particularly sorry to lose my Charleston-made desk.

Even though we had been customers in the past and had held our first wedding reception at the motel, they worried us to pay in advance, so we left after two days. John-Paul insisted that we move to the Golden Eagle Motel on Meeting Street. There we spent three happy weeks. John-Paul took lots of photographs of Natasha and me. He said how much he looked forward to coming 'home' to us after a hard day on the docks.

Father Stringer, while saddened that we had returned to America, was nevertheless very understanding. He was the strong link that bound me to John-Paul, for whom he felt such an affinity. Writing to me he said:

I am praying for John-Paul and your happiness together—but I grieve for your dream of being in England.

Father Stringer and I had chosen some of Mother Rutherford's belongings for the Booth Bay Theatre Museum in Maine, where Franklyn Lenthall, Natasha's godfather, is curator. If nothing else since my visit his letter proved that he had felt well enough to sort some of her precious mementos.

He noted:

She's [Vicky's] done up the Dress and the Cloak and the dear flowery hat, and I've put in the Script *Ring Around the Moon* which you can sell.
I have the scripts of *all* the Marple Films . . . but I don't know *how* I can send those—if it's legal, I mean?
Mrs George Nash of the Vic & Albert Museum was very nice, took all the photos for sorting and will help me similarly with letters when I can bring myself to the bonfire stage.
Leighton House Theatre Museum has accepted the Recital Dress but doesn't want the White Cloak.

As usual there was a message for my husband:

Tell John-Paul I'm sorry but our Gerrards Cross Station waiting-room now has a push-button electric fire!

John-Paul had so enjoyed the waiting-room's coal fire the night our English honeymoon ended.

Both John-Paul and I thought that we would stand a better chance of renting an apartment if I hunted alone. A Black husband, half-black baby and a chihuahua puppy would be a more than formidable obstacle in Charleston! My friend, Dr Robert P. Coggins, a descendant of Robert E. Lee, whom I had met by sheer coincidence, promised to help me in return for helping him build up a collection of American paintings. He told me to try and find a decent apartment, giving his name as a reference.

133

Even so the first attempt to find a home was disastrous. I had agreed to rent a townhouse when at the last minute I was informed by the original tenant that he had decided not to leave. Later it turned out that the owner had heard who I was. He had even called Herman Schindler, owner of a very famous antique shop, to verify the fact. Why, I shall never know. He could have called me personally.

Finally, in desperation, while visiting Ritchia Atkinson, I asked if there might not be an apartment to rent in her building. Once a very high-class apartment block, it had somehow deteriorated. The young White manageress took my deposit at once.

I moved the few remaining antique furnishings, which I had stored before my departure, into the tiny two-room apartment. The bigger room I divided into a sitting-room and bedroom by constructing bookcases down the middle. We had no bed, so I borrowed two old mattresses from the manageress. It really didn't bother me where I slept, as long as it was with my husband.

My mother-in-law didn't share my opinion. She disapproved of our sleeping on the floor and informed me that she had forbidden John-Paul's teenage brother to tell the rest of the family.

I sold my engagement ring—really gave it away—for just enough to get Natasha a decent cot.

Natasha celebrated her first birthday on 16 October 1972 in our pocket-sized home. She had a cake with one candle and her name on top. I am not a very good cook, so it came from a bakeshop.

The following weeks were happy ones. John-Paul did not dwell on the loss of our home any more. When he was not working for Eddie Richards he was home modelling heads out of wet clay that he dredged up from the river. He usually created from his own imagination. Once he spontaneously reproduced, without foreknowledge, a Black man's head shaped like a mug, whose twin I came across sometime later in Judith Wragg Chases's book, *Afro-American Art and Craft*. He also copied from a photograph I showed him an ancient Nigerian head which one day Natasha will be proud to say her father made.

He became terribly protective of us both and for a time would not even allow us to walk alone to the elevator. We had both been disturbed by a mysterious man who had begun to accost me on the street, once when I was out with the baby and little Annette, Grandmama Evelyn's grandchild. Very unkempt, he had the tired red eyes of a drug addict. Once he followed me into the apartment elevator. Fortunately an old girlfriend of John-Paul's and her escort were fellow passengers so I reached our apartment in safety.

W even entertained a few friends. It was a pleasant interlude. Ritchia was always popping in for a cup of tea ... and there were delicious breakfasts with my beloved Grandmama Evelyn half a block away. It was just like having a mother again. She called me her child and Natasha 'we (meaning our) baby'.

Then Ritchia left hurriedly to join her fiancé in New Orleans, and with her usual generosity gave me everything in her apartment. Little Annette and I had a wonderful time sorting pots, pans, ornaments and clothing.

I was so happy. I was with my husband. We had somewhere to live and I was enjoying Natasha so much.

Everything must have been going too well, for on 11 December tragedy struck again. The telephone rang at 7.20 a.m. John-Paul answered it, and said, 'England . . .'

It was my sister Fay. 'Dad is dead,' she said. 'Do you wish him buried or burned?'

'Buried,' I managed to say.

'Will you be there?'

'Yes,' I replied.

Dr Coggins arranged everything, including my fare, Natasha travelling free. On Sunday we flew to Miami and that night flew back to England. It was bitterly cold upon arrival; a policeman carried Natasha into the bus for me. We took the train down into Kent, where my sister met us at Staplehurst Station where I distinguished myself by catching a shoe on the carriage step. It had to be rescued from the tracks. Fay seemed very pleased to see us and had arranged for us to stay at the George Hotel in Cranbrook, an old coaching inn with marvellous beams. I slept in a bed that had belonged to Queen Victoria's beloved Prime Minister, Benjamin Disraeli. It had a little window at the foot through which Natasha could peep at me from her cot. Confused by the difference in time, she refused to go to sleep until the early hours of the morning. I listened to that same wind which I used to enjoy so much as a child at Sissinghurst.

This was the first time since I became Dawn Langley Hall, and later Mrs John-Paul Simmons, that I had taken part in any family function apart from my English wedding and Natasha's christening. For some reason I felt like the Duchess of Windsor . . . I was chief mourner at a funeral in the same church from where my

beloved Margie had been buried and at which ceremony I had not been even welcome. I had not even
known that she had died.

As I had bought the ground where Margie was
buried and the grave space next to it at the time I had
erected her memorial cross, and as both my sister and
I were adamant that our mother's resting-place should
not be disturbed, we decided that at least Jack would
lie beside her. It wasn't until afterwards that Mrs
Christian Cook told me that the old custom was to bury
unfaithful husbands next to their faithful wives, rather
than on top of them! Our poor faithless father, we
honestly didn't know of any such thing!

On the funeral morning I went to Jack's cottage,
vacuumed the floor, took in the wreaths and listed
them.

I had an elegant black two-piece suit trimmed with
jet beads, a black velvet pillbox hat and tiny veil. Fay
was also in deep mourning because, as she said, 'our
mother believed in it.'

Aunt Emily Louisa, Jack's only living sister, was
there with her husband, Uncle Thomas Snell. They
were both very taken with Natasha, and Aunty said
that Natasha had Grannie Copper's wide forehead and
eyes. They both gave her some silver.

As we drove through the village to Holy Trinity
Church I asked Fay how we should walk. 'We will walk
together,' she pronounced, 'and let the others fall in as
they will.'

Her husband Jim and their sons were waiting by the
church gate. I shook hands with Jim and said, 'You do
look good. You haven't changed a bit.'

'You don't look so bad yourself,' he said, and with

that unexpected note of approval, the prodigal daughter returned home.

My sister had chosen two very nice hymns for the funeral service while the vicar said that our father had made a contribution to village life and that he had a very agile mind. I glimpsed Nigel Nicolson, the author son of V. Sackville-West, Jack's late employer, whom I had last seen when as a child he had attempted to give me a ride on Abdul the Moroccan donkey, but Abdul had objected, throwing me into a bed of thistles. I didn't have a chance to speak to him, however, as Aunty Emily Louisa collapsed as she threw some carnations into the grave. I was holding her.

The vicar was very kind. 'You have come a very long way,' he said. Fay had arranged a nice funeral tea with plenty of sherry at the room over the Bull Inn.

During the service Natasha had been minded by Alfred and Dora Read, close friends of Margie. When I fetched her for the funeral tea Dora had her all ready in a little dress of red velvet with puffed muslin sleeves. She had learned to walk since our return to America the previous September.

Natasha had a great time chasing her second cousin, Kevin Larkin, Fay's grandson, who wasn't at all sure that he wanted such feminine attention.

Aunty Babs and Uncle Ernie Burgess drove us back to the George Hotel where I made Aunty laugh when I said, 'Margie would turn in her grave if she knew they'd preached a sermon on Jack.' Aunty Babs gave Natasha two dear little toy deer for Christmas.

Natasha and I sat up in Benjamin Disraeli's bed until two in the morning munching the apples that my Cousin Peter Burgess had given us after the funeral. He had driven straight to the church from Covent Garden where he had been loading fruit for his business.

We returned to America that Saturday. It was rather a hard flight, with a long stopover in Ireland. John-Paul was very pleased to see us. He hugged me and said, 'I'm never going to let you leave me again.' Then he fell on the floor and foamed at the mouth. I thought he was having a fit. All that night he was spitting. In the morning he seemed quite normal again.

'Don't dress today,' he suggested. 'Let's stay in bed and rest.' I was only too glad to comply after flying to England and back within a week.

I had brought back several family 'treasures', including Margie's most cherished possession, an art nouveau pewter vase decorated with languishing ladies and irises. Also a framed picture of the herb garden seat that Jack had made from old Tudor mantel fragments for V. Sackville-West. He had always been proud of it.

CHAPTER SIX

The Black children in the neighbourhood called me 'Mrs John-Paul', which pleased me very much. It gave me a sense of belonging, for children either like you or they don't. Natasha and I still took our daily walks with the stroller. One woman dubbed me the 'walkenest' lady on the street.

I found living in so small an apartment very confining. All I could see out of the window was a parking lot. For somebody who had been brought up among the fields and woods of Sussex I cannot say that I really liked it.

There was little privacy; the other tenants all wanted to use my telephone, which Dr Coggins had installed to help with the art research I had undertaken for him. I have always been an introvert and I often felt like my cousin Isabel Whitney who used to say when she didn't want to meet somebody: 'I am not on display today.'

It was all right while John-Paul was there, but he had disappeared again and if we saw him for ten minutes in two weeks we would be lucky. His sculpturing materials lay discarded upon a table.

With John-Paul absent I kept my sanity by reading all my favourite books by V. Sackville-West and Virginia Woolf. It was a time of refreshment and regeneration, for I had no inspiration to write myself.

Every morning the bright spot would be a visit to Grandmama Evelyn who was always great fun so long as I didn't broach the subject of men. 'The only man I'm waiting for now is Jesus,' she would remind me, testily. She was very good with Natasha. I wish that I could have taped the Gullah dialect lullabies she used to sing her.

Dr Coggins came for his art safaris, sometimes alone, but usually with Mrs Coggins or a friend. Grandmama Evelyn and Annette would baby-sit for me. It was the only pleasure I had. I enjoyed eating with Dr Coggins in some of the best restaurants in town.

On fine afternoons Natasha and I would search an old abandoned garden next door for seedlings to start a garden in flower-pots. We found some exotic pink lilies and even boasted our own little fig tree.

Letters from England were always bright spots. Father Stringer had decided that the steep hill to Hatfield was not good for his health. He had decided to sell the bungalow and was looking for a house in Hammersmith close to Vicky Lang-Davis's old church. Apparently it all hinged on a mortgage, and he wrote:

> I'm going through rather a beastly mood of fearing I Never *will* get another mortgage and if not *WHAT?* . . . I'm up & down & muddled.

He had been to London:

> I called on Margaret's stand-in, Grace Bridges, who is in a Home in Kensington—I think you must have met her.

The local newspaper had taken a picture on the docks with John-Paul in the foreground. I had sent this to

Father Stringer (without mentioning the frequent disappearances). He commented later:

I also liked the picture of John-Paul and his ship—he does stand well! Quite stole the picture! I love to hear news of him, and do send him my best wishes.

Basil Ashmore, who had directed Mother Rutherford in a play on the island of Malta, had written a review of her autobiography in the *Bucks Examiner*, 26 January 1973. It pleased Father Stringer very much, and he sent me a copy. He had circled one paragraph:

She [Mother Rutherford] provided a many-sided personality to those who really knew her. Strong and pugnacious as a lion when faced with a situation which offended her sense of right and wrong, she was painfully diffident, at times, about the value of her acting.

How right Mr Ashmore was. How she had stood her ground for John-Paul and me.

I had also sent Father Stringer a review of a new biography of Tallulah Bankhead which delighted him, for years before, when they had both been young and Tallulah was the toast of the London stage, he had acted as her stage manager. Years later I had met Miss Bankhead on one of my visits to the novelist Carson McCullers at Nyack, New York. Tallulah liked animals so we had a mutual interest to discuss.

By April the pesty mortgage had not gone through, and he was still at Hatfield. I had written for a particular picture; promptly came the reply:

I've no photo in the house of Mother Rutherford in *Mouse on the Moon* but will search garage when it's a bit warmer! I sent some copies to the V & A Museum.

In the same letter he thanked me profusely for a Noël Coward cutting, which he thought 'quite the best he had seen anywhere.' He went on:

> I was very grieved over his death & Binkie Beaumont's. They had both meant so much in our lives, and I had my first walk-on engagement in the West End in one of Coward's first appearances—*Knight of the Burning Pestle*.

So many of his old friends were leaving life's stage that I felt deeply sorry for him. But he had been promised Mother Rutherford's tombstone for Easter and was impatient to see it in place.

Natasha really enjoyed Easter that year. Remembering how much my sister and I had loved it, and how dear Margie had always ordered our eggs from Tommy Waghorne the Sissinghurst baker, with our names iced on top, I did my best for our child. I took her to the shop on Church Street where 'we dress little girls to look like little girls', buying a lavender smocked dress, with a bonnet of white rosebuds. For my little stepson I found a white linen suit and bow tie. On the way back we found an Easter basket in Woolworth which I filled with toy rabbits, chickens and chocolate eggs. We carried them to Marion Square Park on Easter Sunday.

It was a happy, lazy Sunday spent with Natasha lying between us. At four o'clock John-Paul's mother called to see us and after a visit of two hours I volunteered to walk her home, taking Gussie Mae, the corgi, with us. Leaving Mrs Simmons at her home I decided to walk back through the College of Charleston Campus and down St Philip's Street.

About half-way, and in sight of Charleston Police Station, I had the misfortune to run into the drug addict who had tried so often to talk to me. I passed quickly, without a word, and then felt a hand grab my shoulder. Gussie Mae growled but he kicked her and she ran off, whimpering. Throwing me to the ground, he kicked me in the face, then dragged me behind a derelict house. All I could think was: 'My poor child, what will become of my poor child?'

My face was covered with blood; he tore at my clothes. But God was with me, for a young Black couple suddenly appeared in the alley, causing my attacker to run. The girl tended me while her escort phoned for the police.

I was taken to the county emergency room where my mouth and head had to be stitched. Four of my front teeth were so shattered they had to be extracted. When John-Paul appeared I was in a wheelchair. He was terribly upset. Kneeling beside me he said over and over, 'Oh, no . . . no. . . .',

We later had to visit the police station where they took photographs of me and I was shown mug shots of suspects. None resembled the attacker, whom I could easily have identified. Annette could have done the same, as she was with me on the other day that he had tried to accost me. Vanishing into thin air, I never saw him on the streets of Charleston again.

The police took my new blood-spattered green velvet coat for tests and I have never seen it since. Although they were supposed to have visited the scene of the crime, when I went back to it a week later, I found my white fur hat and a button torn from my coat. Their search had not been very thorough.

I was so very ill that Christmas of 1972 that I was able to drink only through a straw. Friends were exceedingly kind to us. Peter and Marie Schwerin gave us a Christmas tree, Christmas dinner, money, and, best of all, promised us an American sleigh bed. West Grant, my hairdresser, brought us a turkey dinner with all the trimmings and washed the matted blood out of my hair, so that at last I didn't feel like the Bride of Frankenstein. We had a large box of cheeses from Jo Spironello . . . these I feel saved my life as they were easy on my mouth. Earl and Miriam Long brought us an enormous box of goodies, as did the ever-faithful Florence Haskell, who had been so good when baby was born, receiving telephone threats as reward for her Christian kindness. Down the street there was Grandmama Evelyn and her daughter Rosabelle Ten Cents Waites to help bathe and care for Natasha. In spite of all the pain—I was treated by a neurosurgeon, as during the struggle with my assailant a nerve had been pinched at the base of my spine—it was not an unhappy time as I felt a real closeness to John-Paul who cared for us both so lovingly.

In England, Father Stringer was horrified by news of the brutal beating: 'I have written to the British Ambassador giving your name & address and telling of the attack and asking if he can "ginger up" police enquiries,' he wrote.

He was readjusting now to life without Mother Rutherford, and had even been to the theatre which had been so much a part of their lives. He wrote:

I went to Dame Sybil's [Thorndike] Tribute at the Haymarket and people were very nice greeting me. But I could only manage to stay in the dear Theatre for one act.

He even considered taking a small role in a movie, but his heart was troubling him and it was not to be.

His letters helped me keep my sanity as they had always done. Like my Mother Rutherford, he could see only good in John-Paul and me. Marriages, he quite believed, were made in heaven.

I had mentioned Princess Margaret, of whom I had written a biography some years before, and of how I thought she now resembled the young matronly Victoria.

Commenting, he added:

Saying something about Princess Margaret looking like Queen Victoria you enclosed the loveliest cut-out picture of Mother Rutherford—was this a mistake. Or did you want it for one of your collections? I HOPE not—I LOVE IT!!

Of course I meant it for him to keep.

From Louisiana came sad news. Ritchia never married her Louis. He was found murdered, stripped naked, tied to a board and thrown into a bayou.

John-Paul turned up out of the blue in time to take our photographs. I wore the palest pink taffeta dress, a gift from Ritchia Atkinson, set off with a yellow straw Panama hat.

Later my hairdresser told me that one of the County

librarians had seen us and had commented, 'They made a very pretty sight.'

Natasha walked to the park; the farthest she had ever walked.

John Paul had gone by the time we reached home again.

During the summer we enjoyed visits to Captain Glover Hayes, the old sea captain and scholar who lived on Radcliffe Street. John-Paul and I had given him his boxer, Lady. After that it was always 'Captain Glover and his Lady'. The Captain treated Lady like a daughter. Natasha was always intrigued on her visits to his home, especially when he was working at his nets, for although past seventy his still nimble fingers fashioned them beautifully. Then one day we arrived to find that Lady had become a mother. Three of the puppies looked like her, while the smallest was brown and white. The Captain said that Natasha could pick one for herself. She chose the small one and every other day went to see how Nelly, as we had christened her, was doing.

Lady would charge out to greet us. Natasha would say: 'Hello, Lady.' Then she would hold on to her collar and together they would walk indoors. She certainly inherited my love for animals.

Dr Coggins knew that I was not happy in my jail, as he called the apartment, so, in the late summer of 1973, he made it possible for us to purchase the Carrere-Simmons House at 135, Coming Street. It was a house that had known better days but was partially restored with the nicest kitchen I had ever had. There were orange parrots on the wallpaper.

The house dated from 1828, had some Adam features and an iron eagle in the fanlight. Opposite was the same Cathedral Church that had refused Natasha baptism. The Cathedral was floodlit at night so that, especially when it was misty, I could look through the giant elm and imagine myself home in England.

The sleigh bed was duly restored and we moved into our new home at very short notice. I painted the dining-room a lovely daffodil yellow which brought out the beauty of the black Italian marble mantelpiece that had been placed there in mid-Victorian times. The fireplace worked. Best of all, I felt like writing again. Rutherford-Davis was so happy to have a sunny piazza on which to sit! Surely, I thought, they will leave us in peace. . . . Please God, let me work in our own house and not bother anybody.

We were still alone, but it did not matter for John-Paul phoned sometimes. I heard that he was living with the same party again. I pretended not to know. I knew my day would come.

Natasha and I did a little gardening. I would dig the hole and she would push in a hyacinth. We planted some pink and white Roses of Sharon and tended the new iris bed.

Father Stringer was glad that I seemed settled at last. 'I do hope you will be very happy,' he wrote on 7 August. 'What lovely news of Natasha. Her photo is still on our piano.'

Mother Rutherford's stone was in place at last, a beautiful red granite one with exquisite gold lettering. At the foot was the epitaph:

A BLITHE SPIRIT

'Gerrards Cross has got very lonely, . . .' he said in closing. 'NO ONE comes to see us and the Doctors say this big hill is doing me no good.'

He died in his sleep on 30 August.

I was heartbroken. I phoned the docks and John-Paul rushed over to be with me. I knew he would come.

I telephoned Vicky; it was the best I could do.

Gwen Robyn, who had done such a sensitive job helping Mother Rutherford with her autobiography, sent me this description of his funeral:

Dear little Stringer; it was all so Rutherfordish. Vicky splendid in purple and large black hat sitting with the esteemed family Admiral. . . . There were masses of flowers and a touching service. One or two theatrical people, but that was all. . . . At the last moment before I left with Vicky to go to the church she remembered Stringer wanted John Gielgud's letter to be buried with him. I searched through everything but could not find it, and then she remembered that he probably went to bed with it in his pocket and so it would be with him anyway. I wrote G. who sent me a charming letter back. But isn't it like the darlings? The world is a sadder place for their going. Margaret must have been so happy when they lowered him down to her in the graveyard. I can just see her saying to Stringer on his arrival up above: 'Oh dear heart, the cream cakes here are so delicious.'

CHAPTER SEVEN

Things had begun to pick up. The Carrere-Simmons House might not have been everybody's cup of tea, but after the cramped apartment we had vacated it was heaven. There was a modern lavatory, although the bath itself didn't function. Natasha was bathed in one of the two stainless-steel kitchen sinks and loved it. Aunt Martha Whitney's gold swag curtains miraculously fitted the dining-room windows. I hung the painting of faithful Banji over the Empire sideboard that had been made in Savannah. With a new gas heater the large bedroom upstairs was usable and quite adequate for the winter months.

Nelly the boxer was growing up, having a good companion in Daffodil, the German Shepherd puppy, another gift to Natasha, and in Isadora, the chihuahua, but Rutherford-Davis still ruled the roost.

John-Paul might be missing but otherwise we were seemingly at peace. I was writing again. Natasha had plenty of room to play. At the end of the day we walked down to Grandmama Evelyn's for supper.

Mrs Janice McInness, our social worker who had kept a watchful eye upon us ever since the in-laws had threatened to take Natasha and shut me in the State Hospital, was insistent that I apply for food coupons. Then she said I might sit at the typewriter and earn some real money. I would not have to run down town every afternoon with baby in her stroller to sell my personal possessions for a song so as to feed ourselves.

I was still having to eke out our existence by selling what possessions still remained because although John-Paul had been in regular employment with Richards Launch Service for eighteen months he had never allowed us one penny. If he had given us a little food money, then I could have worked on remunerative newspaper articles that would have helped him as well as us. But it was the usual story. By his own admission he was keeping the same woman and her family, giving her eighty dollars a week! Fifteen of these would have been sufficient for the baby and me. *It hurt.*

Thank God I could think of Margie and how she had suffered and won over her adversities with a weak, faithless husband. Through everything she had kept her marriage vows; had never deserted him . . . and I had seen how he had suffered, his legs all crippled up, after she had died.

Now Margie slept in Sissinghurst Churchyard with Jack safely beside her. Sometimes I longed to sleep also, but there could be no rest until my child was properly raised and able to fend for herself.

The first visit to the food stamp office was a revelation for I had never seen so many hungry people in my life! I was interviewed by a militant Black lady who turned out to be one of my readers. She nearly hit the ceiling when I told her that I had sold every bit of jewellery I ever had, with the exception of my wedding ring. By my second visit she had done some investigating of her own and informed me that the lady who was getting my husband's eighty dollars was also on the food stamp and welfare programme.

She was very kind, and saw that Natasha and I were given sixty-six dollars' worth of coupons a month, and that later it was raised to seventy-eight dollars. We could eat meat for a change. I was so grateful. It didn't matter that I was White and my child Black . . . my dear Black militant food stamp lady was true American all through. Right was right. I have met some fine people since I became poor.

The new book could now progress rapidly. We would not be on food coupons for long! I felt so elated. John-Paul called us, usually in the middle of the night when the household where he stayed was asleep. Around Thanksgiving of 1973 he telephoned several times in one evening. He seemed very mixed up. Mr Eddie Richards, his boss, was phoning me to know where he could be found. I could only tell him where I thought he was.

'Those people claim he's not there,' was Mr Richards' reply.

Thanksgiving came and I lit a fire in the black marble fireplace. My American cousin, Isabel Whitney, had taught me to love Thanksgiving, and it is my favourite day of the year. At the old Whitney mansion in New York we used to let the servants retire while we sat around the drawing-room fire toasting marsh-mallows. Then we examined the family collections of antique vinaigrettes, portrait miniatures, and Chinese snuff bottles. Well, at least my own poor child had a marble fireplace, too ironically black.

Annette Waites, Natasha's idol, came to eat with us. She brought her friend Sarah. Neither had seen an open fire before, so it was one Thanksgiving they will always remember.

We had been given a duck which I cooked with English roast potatoes and candied yams. It was a good Thanksgiving although the chair we longed most to be filled was empty.

John-Paul's telephone calls now became increasingly frequent. He seemed to be undergoing some kind of crisis. I called Richard's Launch Service to find out that he had left them two weeks before. It was a shock. John-Paul loves the water and he had seemed so happy working there. That was why I had never legally bothered him for support. I didn't want to make trouble for him on his job, and besides, I loved him too much to take him into court.

Then on the evening of 3 December my world nearly came to an end.

A month before, Suellen Austin, a nationally known antique owner, telephoned me that she was very disturbed on my behalf. She begged me to make the house absolutely secure. 'I have heard that somebody is going to try to kill you,' she said.

I wish I had heeded her warning, but then I had been threatened so often before. Perhaps I should have called the F.B.I., for the local police had never solved the last attack that had taken place.

Somehow I could not believe that anything terrible would happen again. I was sure the unknown 'somebody' would leave me alone. The Warren Street neighbours were kindness itself to Natasha and me, and always recruited me to read the letters of some of the old people who couldn't read or write.

Yet there was still the biggest nightmare of all to come. On that day I was tired. The past few weeks had been trying, as Captain Hayes had fallen sick and, after some days in hospital, had died. John-Paul had not turned up for his funeral and I had felt it very much having to go on my own. I had been looking after Lady, Captain Hayes's boxer, who was not well herself, and had also been working on my new book.

As usual I was filling an extra bottle for Natasha before retiring myself when I heard a crash upstairs. Thinking that Natasha had fallen out of her cot I ran upstairs to find one of the bedroom windows open. The dogs were whimpering behind me, not barking as they would usually have done.

My first thought was that John-Paul had come home as he had done many times before. Thinking he might be hiding, I said, 'Don't frighten me, John-Paul, I'm so weary tonight.'

It wasn't John-Paul who jumped out from behind the door but a complete stranger; a slim young man who grabbed me by the arm. Then I saw that he had a knife! Pulling me towards the cot he held the blade over sleeping Natasha, threatening to kill her!

Nobody will ever know the terror of that moment. All I could think of was my child. The intruder dragged me towards the open window and, when I resisted, twisted my left arm. I heard it snap. Then he punched my face and pushed me, bleeding, through the open window on to the upper piazza. Natasha's quilt was hanging over the rail. Throwing me down he covered my face; then he raped me twice.

When he had finished he ordered me to lie still, saying he would be back. I heard him climb back through the window. I waited a few minutes, then struggled to my feet and by some miracle managed, broken arm and blood streaming down my face, to hoist myself up on to the windowsill. Dropping to the bedroom floor, I ran over to Natasha. Mercifully she was still asleep! I tried to lift her but I couldn't. The dogs seemed dazed and powerless. (Later the police thought the rapist came prepared with a solution to spray in their eyes.) I ran downstairs in my nightgown, making for the police station just a block away.

'Good God!' said a policeman when I opened the door.

They asked me to call John-Paul as next of kin. I called the house of the woman with whom he was living, and he said: 'It serves you right for living in a Black neighbourhood!'

The policeman helping with the call was Black. 'What colour is your husband?' he asked. When I told him, 'Well, it takes all sorts to make a world', was his response.

I returned to the house with a young officer. By that time the effects of whatever substance had been used on the dogs was wearing off; they were barking loudly. Nelly, the boxer, and Daffodil the German shepherd, were rushing up and down the lower piazza. The policeman told me to shut up the dogs before he would come in.

When this was done he carried Natasha downstairs. I noticed that the portable television set was still in the bedroom; that the silver teapot remained on the sideboard; and that my purse was intact on the dining-room table. Evidently robbery had not been the attacker's motive.

We took Natasha in the police car to Grandmama Evelyn's. Then I was taken to the emergency room. Dr John Siegling, a bone specialist, pronounced the arm broken. My nose was also broken and had to be set. My mouth was stitched inside and out. Another doctor examined me for injuries sustained from the raping.

It was a nightmare. I was violently sick. Dr Siegling advised me to go into hospital but I could not leave Natasha. The policeman drove me back to Grandmama Evelyn's where I spent the rest of the night.

The two detectives who arrived the next morning to question me asked if I thought that my husband had instigated the whole thing. Of course I said I did not.

We were quite alone. There was still no news from John-Paul. This time I was so worn, so hopeless, so benumbed that I took much longer to recover my strength. For the first time in her life Natasha was ill, having gone down with flu. She cried for me to pick her up, persisting when I could not. Though the food stamps remained a blessing I felt utterly defeated.

But Natasha had her Christmas after all. James R. Gregg, a salesman with Oxford University Press, and a friend from Isabel's days, sent me the money to get Natasha a rocking-horse. And on Christmas Eve when I was filling her stocking John-Paul returned. The parking lot next door was filled with cars and festive worshippers. It was pouring rain. I thought I heard somebody yell 'Mama!' It was he! We had the happiest Christmas I have ever known. Natasha was so happy to see her father asleep in the old walnut sleigh bed when she awoke next morning. It was the best present of all. Dora Read, who had minded her during Jack's funeral service, had knitted her the most lovely little blue pleated dress, and being Natasha, she had put it on at once. The same with the blue sweater from Cousin Pat. She cleaned her teeth with Mrs Karet's toothbrush that came packed with a rabbit made from face-cloths. Her Aunty Fay, my sister, had sent her a Beatrix Potter jigsaw. She had a lovely time.

While they lay in bed I stuffed a duck with oranges and the same kind of breadcrumb stuffing that my Sussex grandmother had made. We lit a fire in the dining-room and all sat down at table together, Natasha in her Spanish high chair.

John-Paul said grace . . . and I didn't even have to ask him.

New Year came and he was still with us. He sent some neighbourhood boys for fireworks. We all three sat on the marble steps to watch them. I remember thinking, 'Why, oh why can't the whole world stop now while I am so happy!'

Yet we both knew that we were living in Charleston on borrowed time. Natasha and I would, for our own safety, have to leave. But John-Paul was a man. His pride would never let him run away.

Friends and relatives were horrified at this latest attack on my person. Dr Siegling had told me the worst. My left arm would never be straight again, for in addition to the break, the ligaments had been badly torn. For the rest of my days it would be crippled. For five minutes I felt badly about it, then I thought of what Mother Rutherford would have said: 'But dear heart, you can always wear long sleeves.'

I was now determined that my daughter should be happy even if it meant my separation from the only man I would ever love.

From Italy came a letter, dated 20 January 1974, from Natasha's actor-godfather, Anthony Dawson, who was about to leave for America to star with Richard Burton in a film about the Ku Klux Klan.

'You really are nuts to just keep on living in that area when all you get is knocked about. It's not worth the fight to live among idiots.'

That was the cold-water douche of common sense.

CHAPTER EIGHT

Grandmama Evelyn often told me: 'God is not asleep.'
She was right.

The opportunity arose for me to buy the historic
President Van Buren House at Catskill, New York.
Built in 1797, an official state historic marker in the
garden tells how the young Martin Van Buren, destined
to become the eighth President of the United States of
America, was married there to Hannah Hoes in 1807.

It seemed poetic justice that having lost two houses
in Charleston and, through force of circumstances,
having to sell a third for our own safety's sake, I should
now have one of national importance. We could open
several rooms to the public as a house museum;
Natasha would grow up with a sense of history.

James Gregg drove us up to see our new home on a
snowy February day. Dr Coggins, as always, generously
helped me.

Back in Charleston, Gussie Mae, the faithful Welsh
corgi who had been kicked so brutally by the drug-
addict attacker of Christmas, 1972, suffered a ruptured
uterus after giving birth to puppies. I felt so sorry for
her. It reminded me of what I had gone through myself
in the now dim days before I became Dawn. When she
died two weeks later, Natasha said, 'Gussie is with Baby
Jesus.'

As an act of humanity and compassion, Alice Conroy,

wife of Charleston's Police Chief John F. Conroy, who now owned Spicers House, allowed me to retrieve my faithful Jackie's ashes. They now rest in our garden beneath a mountain at Catskill.

John-Paul has a little house by his beloved river and as the Hudson runs by my door I will always think of him when we are apart. One day he may even sink his pride and join us.

As he helped load Natasha, Rutherford-Davis, our other dogs and my personal belongings into the station wagon that was to take us to the North and safety, my eyes were full of tears.

'Was I a good wife?' I asked.

'The best,' he said.

I shall always believe he meant it.